A Hundred Years Ago

The beginnings of Girl Guiding in Nottinghamshire

with all good wishes

Rowena-Edlin-White

Rowena Edlin-White

Oct '09

smallprint
for Girlguiding Nottinghamshire,
with assistance from the Jessie Spencer Trust

Published for Girlguiding Nottinghamshire
16, Burton Road, Carlton, Nottingham, NG4 3DF
www.girlguidingnottinghamshire.org.uk
Charity No. 503168
by smallprint
2009

smallprint is an imprint of *Woolgatherings*,
11, Frederick Ave, Carlton, Nottingham NG4 1HP, England, UK
0115-9873135

ISBN 978-1-900074-22-3

Printed by Hassall & Lucking Ltd.
Long Eaton NG10 1HD

Contents

Acknowledgements

With grateful thanks to all who helped with this book, especially:
Myra Chilvers for suggesting I write it, Sue Davies for patiently fielding all my queries, Miss E. Hawkins who allowed me access to the YWCA Archive at Warwick, Karen Taylor at Guide Headquarters in London and Helena Pielichaty, curator of the Collingham & District Local History Collection. Girlguiding Midlands archivists Margaret Outram (Lincolnshire) and Mavis Stanley (Leicestershire) were also most helpful.

I would like to thank the Trease, Watkins and Hawthorne families of Nottingham, and Jan Allton, Peter Blatherwick, Cynthia Charter, Ivy Chilvers, Margaret Cooper, Pam Fogg, Eileen Foster, Yvonne Harris and Eileen Harvey for providing photographs and additional material from personal collections.

Extract from *A Whiff of Burnt Boats* by Geoffrey Trease is used by permission.

Girlguiding Notinghamshire gratefully acknowledges the support of the Jessie Spencer Trust.

Foreword

Celebrating one hundred years of Guiding is a wonderful thing to be able to do, and an opportune moment to look back to the very beginnings of the movement here in Nottinghamshire. Movements consist of people, and the story of these people - mostly women - who had a vision for something different for girls and young women in the region, is an inspiring story - one which might be told around the camp fire to encourage the Guides and Guiders of the 21st Century.

It is especially encouraging to realise that these women, from the whole social spectrum at a time when such things mattered far more than they do today, were very much like ourselves; they saw a good thing and seized it boldly for the common good. Wives and daughters of clergy, teachers and factory workers joined hands with honourables and ladyships to build a better future for Nottingham girls through the "game" of Guiding – and much fun was had along the way!

Much of the material in this book comes from the treasure trove of records, photographs, log books and other memorabilia in the Nottinghamshire Girl Guide Archives at Carlton, chosen with the generous advice of archivist Sue Davies. Karen Taylor, at Guide Headquarters in London, also gave valuable help, delving into their records to fill in some of the gaps. So too did the keepers of many smaller collections scattered around the country who gave me access to their resources. Meeting and interviewing several former Guiders who are close to their own centenaries was also a rare privilege which I shan't forget.

However, like most researchers, I wanted to find some things that weren't already on record at either national or local level – early record-keeping was often sketchy – and this I think I have managed to do. One intriguing line of enquiry led me to the YWCA Archive in the Modern Records Collection at the University of Warwick, where I found clues to the very first Guide Company in Nottingham and much period ephemera besides.

I should explain the time-scale of the book: it would have been impossible to cram a hundred years into as many pages and do my subject any kind of justice, so I made a decision to stick to the very beginnings of the movement, and to finish in 1932 with the coming-of-age celebrations at Southwell Minster and Norwood Park. At twenty-one, the Guides were well able to stand on their own feet and face the future with confidence.

There are still gaps in this account. I have only been able to use the material available and if you, the reader, know of other accounts and collections, do please contact Sue Davies. And if I have misattributed any photos or got any of my facts horribly wrong, do please let us know – consider this book a work in progress!

Rowena Edlin-White, September 2009

Long Row Central, where the first Girl Guide company in Nottingham began

1. The girls invade the pitch – national beginnings

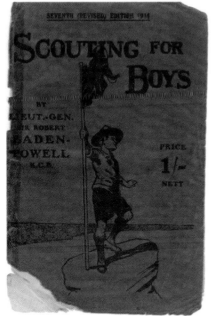

The birth of the Girl Guide movement is well known. The story of how a dozen determined girls turned up uninvited to the first big Scout Rally at Crystal Palace on 4th September 1909, and pleaded with Sir Robert Baden-Powell to let them be Scouts too, is the stuff of legend!

Seventy-five years later, Sybil Canadine, a vicar's daughter from Camberwell, who was one of those girls, described how she and her friends had watched the local Boy Scout troop going off to have "fun and games" and had longed to join in with their activities. The Scout Master suggested that they might follow the boys at a discreet distance and copy what they did. The girls became so keen that they were determined to attend the Rally, in spite of having no tickets. They made themselves uniforms from items found in the church jumble box, borrowed khaki shirts and hats, dyed old sheets for scarves and made woggles from broken shoe-laces. They then walked six miles – in the rain – to Crystal Palace, ignoring the laughter and derision from passers-by.

When they reached Crystal Palace the Rally had already begun, but they simply marched purposefully through the gates and nobody stopped them! Twelve girls among 11,000 boys were bound to be noticed, however, and at lunch time Baden-Powell himself came over to speak to them. They told him they wanted to be Scouts like their brothers and begged him to form a company for girls. He was so impressed he promised to think about it and allowed them to take part in the march-past. Three months later, the Camberwell Scout Master brought them the exciting news that Baden-Powell had decided to form the "Girl Guides", and the movement was officially begun.

Those intrepid girls certainly brought matters to a head, but of course they had already been "scouting" for some time, as had girls all over the country. Girls were reading their brothers' copies of *Scouting for Boys*, and wanted some of the action for themselves. The time was right: middle-class women and girls of the period were ready for something more adventurous than staying indoors and looking decorative; and their working-class sisters, some of whom had been earning their own livings since the age of twelve or thirteen, also longed for healthy outdoor activities and the opportunity to belong to something with a purpose. The Girl Guides would be a place where girls of all classes and education could meet on an equal footing.

Baden-Powell had already been mulling over the possibility of an organisation for girls, encouraged by his mother, Henrietta, and elder sister Agnes. They had urged him forward with his Scouts and could see some of the advantages girls might also gain from a similar movement. Other people thought so, too. Educator Charlotte Mason, founder of the Parents National Education Union (PNEU) movement, had read Baden-Powell's earlier book, *Aids to Scouting*, which was based on his work with boys in South Africa during the Boer War, and thought that younger children could benefit from it. In 1905 she put it on her school syllabus and PNEU Girl Scouts were formed soon afterwards. So one might make a case for Guides being in existence even before the famous camp on Brownsea Island in 1907 from which the Boy Scouts emerged. It was certainly true that by the time of the Crystal Palace Rally, some 6,000 girls from all over the country had already taken it upon themselves to register as "Boy Scouts".

By November 1909 the scheme for Girl Guides was underway, but Baden-Powell approached it with caution: girls were not boys, and there was the danger of public opposition on the grounds that they would all be turned into tomboys! The idea of women and girls in uniform was also repugnant to many people. Guiding was therefore promoted as training for "future wives and mothers of character", with traditional womanly skills like nursing and cookery emphasised. Many girls must have been disappointed to be relegated to genteel domesticity, and forced to change their patrol totems from tigers, leopards and the like, to the names of flowers! However, many of their badge tests such as life-saving, signalling, gymnast and electrician remained the same as the boys', and being allowed to learn these skills was to prove both useful and liberating.

In 1910 Agnes Baden-Powell was appointed first President of the Girl Guides and by May, a Committee was in place, based at Scout Headquarters in London. Miss Margaret Macdonald, who was previously Assistant Secretary at Scout HQ, became first secretary to the Guides, a position she was to hold until 1919. Other Committee members were Miss Beatrice Swaine (Hon. Sec.), Mrs Stewart Mackenzie (Hon. Treasurer) and Mrs William Paget (Chair). Proper registration of companies began and the Guides became official.

Some time that same year, without any great fanfare, the 1st Nottingham Company was formed on the premises of the YWCA Institute.

2. Meanwhile, back in Nottingham....

Local newspapers had begun to report on the progress of the Boy Scout movement from about 1909, gradually showing an increased interest in its activities; but the first inkling that such activities might spread to the county's girls appeared in the *Nottingham Evening Post*, December 18th 1909.
A letter headed "Lord Meath and the Girl Scouts" was published, which included these sentiments:

> "We must as a race prove our worthiness, or we may rest assured that in accordance with the wise dispensation of Providence, we shall be displaced, and rightly displaced from the seats of privilege and of power.
> "A thorough national arousing, a determination on the part of the mass of British men and women – aye, and of British boys and girls – to put aside self and to seek the best interests of the community, can only save us from the moral decay which has preceded the fall of all previous empires. I recognise in the scout movement an effectual means towards this end, but in so much as girls need as much as boys the stimulus of a wholesome discipline to strengthen moral fibre, I trust it will not be long before we see a girls' scout movement developing on lines suitable to the female sex.
> "Let us train up our boys and girls to be God-loving, and God-fearing, to be true to duty, law-abiding, hard-working, not afraid of pain and discomfort, obedient, and respectful to lawful authority, loyal, patriotic, and self-sacrificing, and the nation and empire need have no fear for the future."

Perhaps this was just the kind of encouragement which was needed? Recreational provision for girls had been on the public agenda in Nottingham for years: Girls' Evening Homes, The Girls' Friendly Society, Young Women's Christian Association (YWCA) and The Girl's Diocesan Association were just a few societies which tried to do their best for working-class girls, as well as young women from a more privileged background who were encouraged to help lead and organise them. There had not really been any organisation where girls from across the class divide might meet on an equal footing with common aims and aspirations, and Girl Guides seemed to be the answer.

1st Nottingham (YWCA) Company is on the record books from 1911, but anecdotal evidence points to it having existed before this date (records were rather sketchy in the early days). One of the earliest references to their existence appeared in the YWCA's *Our Outlook* magazine in December 1912, when a 1st prize of two shillings and sixpence was awarded to Maude Birkin of 1st Nottingham Company (YWCA) Girl Guides for the best selection of scripture texts illustrating the ten points of the Guide Law. Elsie Burton from the same Company was also highly recommended.

Miss Maude Andrews was Captain. She was employed as Superintendent at the YWCA Institute at 30 Long Row Central and it is very probable the first company met on those premises. The Institute occupied premises in Long Row Chambers between Hepworth's and G. Dean, Tailor (above what is currently Schuh Footwear), and in 1910 had 450 members: 300 Seniors, 80 Juniors and 70

Intermediates. The first Guides would have been drawn from the Intermediate section (girls over 14) and when Brownies were introduced later, these were recruited from the Juniors, with the result that a girl had to remain a Brownie until her 14th year. This discrepancy was ironed out around 1917 when the YWCA Guides came into line with the mainstream movement (see box).

The YWCA Hostel occupied the Marshall Tallard house on Castle Gate from March 1910, remaining until 1913, when, along with the Institute, they moved permanently into purpose-built premises at 40-42 Shakespeare Street. Miss Andrews moved with them as Superintendent, remaining until at least 1925.

1st Nottingham Y.W.C.A. Guides

Photograph from *Our Outlook*, 1914

The YWCA as an organisation did not officially embrace Guiding until 1914 and 1st Nottingham Co. was well established by then. By 1920 there were at least three more YWCA companies in Nottingham – 1st B, 1st C, and 3rd Nottingham. 52nd Nottingham (YWCA) followed in 1926.

One of the first reports of Nottingham Girl Guides on parade at a Royal occasion appeared in *Our Outlook*, August 1914. The Royal visit took place on 23rd June and the presence of the Guides obviously caused favourable comment:

"The YWCA B-P Girl Guides were up betimes, for a great day had come in their existence. They were to have a share in lining the route for the King and Queen as they passed through the streets of the town. 45 Guides to be dressed, and brushed and straightened and smartened. But when ready and lined up outside the home for the march to the Forest they presented a pleasing sight. They came somewhat as a surprise to the people of the town, who erroneously persisted in calling them "Girl Scouts," if not "Boy Scouts". By their general smartness, quiet demeanour, and good behaviour they won many complimentary remarks from the crowd through which they passed on their home-ward journey. Best of all, the Queen looked their way and smiled, smile answering smile, as they gave their curtsy, followed by a salute. The Queen of England, great in the land, loved and reverenced by her people, had smiled upon them!

"I promise to be loyal to God and the King," thus said the Guides on the day of their enrolment. The loyalty will be the warmer for that smile, the country better for the loyalty. Thus do our beloved King and Queen sow the seeds of kindliness among their people, gathering in the ripe reward of love and trust."

This is one of the earliest photographs of 1st Nottm. (YWCA) Company, taken on the steps of University College, Shakespeare Street, in 1917. It shows Captain (Miss Maude Andrews, centre), Lieutenants, Patrol Leaders and Seconds. Another photo taken on the same occasion (see p. 33) shows that it was a flourishing Company of more than 50 Guides and 12 Brownies.

Before long, other companies were springing up, some attached to existing organisations like the YWCA and Girls' Friendly Society, to schools and even to businesses such as I. & R. Morley, hosiery manufacturers. But mostly they were connected to churches and chapels. Many of the early Guiders were wives or daughters of ministers and parish clergy. Guiding was eagerly embraced as a movement likely to be of benefit to the girls in the parish. Apart from 1st Nottm. (YWCA) Co., some of the earliest companies formed were 2nd Nottm. (St Peter's, Old Radford) Co. in 1914; 3rd Nottm. (Castle Gate) Co. in 1915; 4th Nottm. (Hyson Green) and 6th Nottm. (St Leodegarius) Companies, both 1916. 8th Nottm. (St Mary's), 10th Nottm. (St Catharine's) and 11th Nottm. (All Saints) Companies were all begun in 1917.

EYEWITNESS: Ivy Chilvers nee Clarke (born 1910)

Ivy, who is Meadows-born and bred, originally attended the Railway Mission on Traffic St. Around the age of 11 she began attending the Sunday School at Castle Gate Congregational Church, where she joined 3rd Nottingham Guides:

"Lady Readett-Bayley came to visit us – I suppose today you'd call it assessing us. We had First Aid and she volunteered to lay down... I don't think she was going to be resuscitated or anything like that. The first thing I did was to try and remove her hat and that put her in a panic! We didn't really like to touch her ... perhaps she expected us just to point at her and describe what we would do but she certainly did not want to be manhandled by me!"

3rd Nottm. Company was led briefly by Ruth Quibell to be followed by Miss Armitage who became Mrs Evison, and in 1926 by Sylvia Reddish who became Sylvia Hawthorne after her marriage in 1928 and remained Captain until 1935.

YWCA Guiding really took off when Miss Helen Malcolm responded to an address given by Miss Mollie Lyne at the YWCA Swanwick Conference in 1912, and became determined to pioneer Girl Guides within the YWCA. Companies were affiliated to the "Baden-Powell Girl Guides" as they were then called, and retained their right to appoint their own officers. In actual fact, Miss Malcolm was to be responsible for training many early Guiders across the whole movement. YWCA Guides differed slightly from their mainstream sisters: in addition to their enrolment promise of loyalty to the God and the Sovereign, helpfulness to others and obedience to the Guide Law, they also promised to read a portion of the Bible every day. This "4th Promise" became something of an issue, when in 1917 Baden-Powell requested the YWCA Guides to come into line with the main movement. After much discussion, they did so, retaining the 4th Promise as a bye-law and giving up their own divisional officers.

This is to Certify that

The Third Nottingham
Registered under the B.P.P.F. Headquarters, Clizah Scar.

Company of B.P. Girl Guides

is duly registered at Headquarters

Signed

Agnes Baden-Powell President

Date November 25ᵗ 1915

The earliest surviving Registration Certificate, 3ʳᵈ Nottm. (Castle Gate) Co. November 25ᵗʰ 1915

3. The Nottingham pioneers

Records and personal information for these women is uneven and, inevitably, some early pioneers may have been over-looked or misrepresented, for which I apologise. More early Guiders will be found scattered throughout the book under the "Eyewitness" headings, and are able to speak for themselves.

Maude Andrews (1874-1957)

Agnes Maude Andrews was the Pioneer of Pioneers - the first enrolled Guider of the first Nottingham Girl Guide company, 1st Nottingham Baden-Powell Girl Guides (YWCA) Co., circa 1910/11. Little is known about her life before Guiding except that she had been employed by the YWCA in Nottingham from at least 1905 as Superintendent of the Institute on Long Row. She remained working for the YWCA until about 1925 when she was Division Captain, then moved to the Robert Wilkinson Smith Memorial Homes in Chestnut Grove where she lived for the rest of her life. Maude Andrews remained active in Guiding for many years, appearing on photographs as late as 1944. She died on 19th December 1957 and no death notice or obituary appears to have been published locally. Her ashes were buried in the Church Cemetery on 10th January 1958, apparently without any of the ceremonial which was surely her due.

EYEWITNESS: Eileen Foster (born 1909)

"Miss Andrews was the first Guide Captain. [They] used to do a play with Miss Andrews where the Guides used to come and rescue some children from a burning building... and they used to come through the crowd of people with poles and they used to put two poles together and their belts to make a stretcher and they used to take their ties off for the bandages and they showed us [how] every piece of their uniform could be used in an emergency."

[See Stretcher Party illustration from *How Girls Can Help* on next page.]

Stretcher Party

Edith M. Blagg (1892-1965)

In 1918 Edith Blagg was Captain of 17th Nottingham (St Matthew's) Guide Company. From 1924-51 she was District Commissioner for Nottingham Central and, in 1957, received a Good Service Award.
From 1937-47 she was Warden of Elton Camp.

Edith Blagg's Log Books of 17th Nottingham Rangers are a mine of information about camps in Britain and abroad, including the early days of Elton Camp, but reveal little information about herself.

Her sister, **Frances Blagg**, was Lieutenant of 1stB Nottingham (YWCA) Co. from 1918.

Agnes Boden (1895-1967)

Agnes Leila Mildred Boden was born in Sutton, Surrey, eldest of three daughters of Canon John Charles Boden who was Rector of Nuthall from 1918. Agnes had been involved in Guiding before the family moved to Nuthall, as she is listed as Captain of 1st North Wingfield Company in 1917.

In 1920/21 1st Nuthall Company was formed and Agnes was Captain for 22 years, assisted by her sister, **Dorothy Boden**, as Lieutenant. She also led 15th Nottingham Rangers 1926-27.

Throughout a long and distinguished career in Guiding she held office as Division Commissioner for Nottingham Castle (1920-25); Secretary for Nottingham Castle (1920-32); District Commissioner for Nottingham South District (1926-34); Division Secretary for Nottingham Forest (1927-34); Division Commissioner for Nottingham Forest (1932-45 & 1955- 62); and Assistant County Commissioner for Nottinghamshire (1942-55). She was awarded a Medal of Merit in 1945.

EYEWITNESS: Dora Ambrose (born c.1910)

"About 1924 Miss Boden started a company in Narrow Marsh [44th Nottm. Leenside], one of the poorest areas of.Nottingham. Miss Boden had gradually acquired sufficient uniforms from various sources, to equip each girl with a uniform. These had to be taken to the school room meeting place for each meeting so each child could be really a Guide. Then they had to be taken off and given back to Miss Boden to bring back to Nuthall. The reason was that, from earlier experience, no uniform was ever returned if taken home. Quite frequently these uniforms were washed at the Rectory, and the following Nuthall Guide meeting was spent by the girls sewing on buttons, stripes etc. and doing needful repairs. During the summer the Narrow Marsh Guides would be invited to spend a day in Nuthall with the Guides there. They travelled on the Ripley tramcar and referred to it as 'a day in the country'."

44th Leenside Company; Captain Peggy Barrows.

(From an interview in 1989. Dora was only the fifth Guide to be enrolled in 1st Nuthall Co., by Lady Maud Rolleston, at the early age of 10.)

Miss Boden worked as Clinical Secretary of the Nottingham Cripples' Guild from 1933 until it became a part of the NHS as the Nottingham Orthopaedic Clinic. During the War she served with the Red Cross at the City Hospital. Recommending her for an award in recognition of her services to social work in Nottingham District, the Chief Orthopaedic Surgeon of the Midlands, Mr Malkin, wrote, "She has never spared herself in any way and has been invaluable,"- an accolade which could equally be applied to her unstinting commitment to Guiding.

A member of the Soroptomists, she was house-mother of one of their homes for the elderly for many years. She was also responsible for organising the Nottingham Centenary Pageant on 30th March 1957 and was awarded the MBE in June 1957 in the Queen's Birthday Honours (see photo on right).

Agnes Boden died suddenly on 7th November 1967.

> "We shall miss her very much, for her loyalty, keenness, commonsense, and her willingness to undertake any job that would help the Trefoil Guild, and Guiding, was outstanding. Many of us were present at her funeral service at All Saints on Monday 13th at 1pm. Also present were her Red Cross friends and many Guides and ex-Guides led by the County Commissioner Mrs Owen Walker. The Guides formed a guard of honour for her."
> (Minutes of the Trefoil Guild 1966-90)

Ella Gem (1862-1930)

Isabella Howard Gem was the eldest daughter of Rev. Thomas Gill, Chaplain of The Embassy Church in Paris. It was as the wife of Rev. Canon Hubert Arnold Gem, Vicar of All Saints from 1888 and, from 1913, St Peter's, Old Radford, that she became involved in Guiding. A born organiser, Mrs Gem was concerned to draw together the many isolated workers for girls and young women in the Diocese in order that their influence might be more effective. After her death, Lady Laura Ridding, wife of the first Bishop of Southwell, bore witness to, "the splendid service given by Ella Gem, the faithful servant of God," noting that,

> "She ungrudgingly threw herself into the effort... the demand on her time, strength and capabilities were incessant, but she responded triumphantly to them; and her never-failing helpfulness, gentle winning courtesy and consideration for others; her unselfishness, sincerity of intention, with the absence of fuss, and her quiet power impressed."

Ella Gem was an enthusiastic member of several women's groups in the County, including the Mothers' Union, Women's League, National Union of Women Workers and the Linen Guild connected with Harlow Wood Hospital, and much in demand as a speaker and leader.

She was involved in Girl Guides almost from the beginning of the movement in Nottingham and was Division Commissioner for 12 years, retiring in 1928, two years before her death. In 1929 she was awarded a Medal of Merit for good service to the Movement.

She died on 5th January 1930, aged 68 and Agnes Boden described her funeral:

> "It was with very real affection that Guiders and Guides from all parts of the city lined the path to her last resting place [the Rock Cemetery] and placed a cushion of flowers in the form of a trefoil by her side. Her bodily presence has passed from us but her influence never will and we are proud to think that we have been able to help her in however small a way in the cause of Guiding which was very near the heart of our Guide Mother. To her will always belong the credit of founding the Girl Guide movement in Nottingham which now comprises 76 companies and over 3,000, who wear either the Trefoil or Brownie badges."

Mrs Gem didn't exactly *found* the movement in Nottingham, but she was one of the first Division Commissioners after those posts were created and her considerable organisational skills did much to promote Guiding locally, causing her to be affectionately named, "Guide Mother". Her daughter, **Dorothy Gem**, taught at Broadgate School in The Park and helped run the Guide Company there.

> ***The Guide* April 3 1926**
> "Nottingham City, which for 11 years has been one Division, has recently been divided into three, and Mrs Gem, who has been Div. Comm. for all those 11 years, has taken over one of the new divisions. In order to show their gratitude in a small measure, all the Guiders and Guides, Rangers and Brownies in the City subscribed towards a case containing two hair brushes, two clothes brushes, a mirror and comb in tortoiseshell and silver, as a Christmas present to their retiring Commissioner, and 6 Patrol Leaders for whom lots had been drawn, made the presentation on December 19th. Mrs Gem has been Commissioner ever since Guides first started in Nottingham, and has watched 58 Companies grow up in the city. Of these, only 4 have definitely been disbanded. All the Guides of the city are most grateful to her for her untiring efforts on their behalf and the two divisions which she is leaving will miss her very much."

Hermione Harcourt-Vernon (1889-1943)

Evelyn Hermione Harcourt-Vernon was the youngest daughter of Edward Evelyn Harcourt-Vernon and his 2nd wife, Grace Fitzherbert, of Grove Hall, East Retford.

She was County Commissioner 1920-26.

Miss D. Lester (dates unknown)

Miss Lester was sister of Rev. J.M.F. Lester, who was Vicar of St Catharines's, St Ann's Well Road, 1914-32. She was Captain of 10th Nottingham (St Catharine's) Company which was begun in 1917 and was successful in winning both the Company Relay Swimming Shield for Notts. Girl Guides and the St Cecilia Cup for Music for 1921/22, and the Shield again for 1922/3 (seen in photo, left). Little is known about Miss Lester except that she was one of the earliest Guiders in the area.

Lady Sibell Pierrepont (1892-1968)

Lady Sibell was the daughter of Charles William Sydney Pierrepont, 4th Earl Manvers, and his wife Helen nee Shaw-Stewart. She inherited Holme Pierrepont Hall from her brother Evelyn and in 1923 married Hubert Davys Argles.
She was County Commissioner for Nottinghamshire from 1916 and County Vice President in the late 'twenties and early 'thirties.

Winifred Anna Cavendish-Bentinck, Duchess of Portland (1863-1954)

The Portlands were involved in many philanthropic initiatives in the County. They were not only generous benefactors, but took a personal interest in the people they helped. The glamorous, charismatic Duchess was particularly concerned for the welfare of women and girls, so it is no surprise that she also lent her energies to the Girl Guide movement from its early days. As for many of the organisations she supported, the Duchess regularly threw open the grounds of Welbeck Abbey to groups of Girl Guides and the report below describes a visit in 1923:

Mansfield & District Whitsuntide Weekend Camp in stables at Welbeck, courtesy of Her Grace the Duchess of Portland. Miss Evelyn Royce, District Commissioner, acted as Commandant assisted by Miss Marjorie Alcock and Miss Moakes (Worksop).

"The Guides actually slept in the rooms over the stables but all the cooking was done out of doors... On Sunday [they] attended service at the private chapel of the Abbey. Nothing could have exceeded the kindness of the Duchess, who gave the Guides permission to go where hey liked in the gardens, and did everything possible for their comfort... The camp was visited several times by the Duchess, Lady Victoria Wemyss and members of the house party, two of whom, being Guiders, inspected the camp one day." (*The Guide* June 30 1923)

The Duchess was the first County President from 1916 until her death in 1954, when she was succeeded by her daughter-in-law, **Ivy, Duchess of Portland**.

Ruth Quibell (1901-1989)

Ruth Quibell was born at Shalem Lodge, Newark, and began Guiding in 1914 as a Patrol Leader at her boarding school, Queenwood Ladies' College, Eastbourne, where their Commissioner was Lady Shackleton, wife of the famous explorer. She was a member of 3rd Nottingham (Castle Gate) Co. circa 1915 and records suggest she was even acting as Captain at this period, though she was only about fifteen at the time. It is certainly the case that she became Captain of 3rd Newark Company in 1919 at the age of eighteen. 3rd Newark Co. was closely connected with the Methodist Church, but was not a closed company. She is acknowledged as a pioneer of Guiding in Newark, and often held meetings in the garden of her home. She was District Commissioner 1930-37 and one of the first Camp Advisors in the County.

Guiding was by no means her only interest: she led Women's Fellowship and Sunday School at Charles Street Methodist Church and was President of the National Sunday School Union in 1964. She supported the appointment of women ministers and, at the age of 76, qualified as a local preacher herself. She also served as a magistrate on the Newark Borough Bench in 1948.
In 1934 she married Douglas Pursey Blatherwick, a prominent Methodist and author. He was Mayor of Newark in 1962 and 1963 and Mrs Blatherwick served as Mayoress for two years.

In later years, Mrs Blatherwick devoted her energies to the provision of improved accommodation for the elderly and to the Southfield House complex of warden-assisted flats, which was opened by Princess Anne in 1971. She was President of Newark Age Concern and involved in many other campaigns and initiatives for the betterment of her community. In 1982 she was awarded a well-deserved OBE.

Lady Audrey Readett-Bayley (1883-1977)

Lady Readett-Bayley was born Audrey Cecil Turney, daughter of Sir John Turney, the leather manufacturer, who was a great friend of General Booth of the Salvation Army. In 1903 she married Henry Dennis Readett-Bayley, the second son of Thomas Bayley JP of Lenton Abbey and Langar Hall. Henry was a coal owner with three pits, including Gedling Colliery, who was knighted in 1918.

They had three daughters who were all involved in Guiding: **Hester Spencer** of Ramley House, Pennington; **Barbara Munt**, who was at Broadgate School in The Park with Dorothy Gem, and Captain of 1st Beeston (St Mary's) Guide Co., becoming Division Commissioner for Beeston; and **Diana Sells** (see right). They also had one son, Tom.

Lady Readett-Bayley drove ambulances in Belgium and France in the 1st World War and she and her husband were active in various areas of war work, supported by the miners who agreed to donate one penny for every ton of coal they excavated. Altogether, they contributed the staggering sum of £180,000. After the War, Lady Readett-Bayley served as a Magistrate. She was also responsible for beginning the W.R.V.S in Nottinghamshire and was active in Women's Institute and Mothers' Union.

A committed Guider, she became County Commissioner in 1926. On her retirement from Guiding in 1944, a presentation was made to her at a large rally held at the Manning School.

Lady Readett-Bayley died on 4th May 1977 aged 94, St George's Hospital Milford-on-Sea.

Lady Readett-Bayley on the occasion of her presentation, with the Chief Guide and Miss Andrews, 1944.

Lady Maud Rolleston (1859-1949)

The Sheriff of Nottm., unknown, Sir Lancelot & Lady Maud Rolleston and Lady Readett-Bayley, 1934.

Born Lady Charlotte Emma Maud Dalzell, Maud's mother was lady-in-waiting to Queen Victoria.

She married Col. Lancelot Rolleston in 1882 and came to live at Watnall Hall. Lady Maud was an excellent artist, author and an intrepid traveller.

Her husband was Lieut. Colonel of the South Notts. Hussars, a volunteer yeomanry cavalry company that served in the Boer War, where Sir Robert Baden-Powell distinguished himself. Like many another aristocratic officer's wife, Lady Maud and her companion, Nurse "Nan" Beaver, followed him to South Africa to help nurse the troops, and opened a convalescent home at Kimberley. When Sir Lance was seriously wounded she appealed to Lord Kitchener (who thoroughly disapproved of ladies at the front) and got his permission to travel behind the enemy lines, where she waited for several weeks at Bloemfontein and Kroonstad before being reunited with her husband. She and Nan nursed him for nearly two months until he was fit to travel home. She wrote about her harrowing experiences in *Yeoman Service* (1901), an extraordinary account as much for the social details ("Our clothes were all very shabby and our hearts very sore, but our manners were beautiful," she wrote!) as for the military interest.

Lancelot Rolleston was knighted in 1911. He began Scouts in Watnall and became County Scout Commissioner. Lady Maud had a keen social conscience, running the local Sunday School and founding the Women's Institute in Watnall in 1927. She was awarded the CBE in 1919 and was only the second woman to be a Magistrate in Nottingham. As her husband was involved with Scouting, she similarly became involved with Guides and it is known that she served as Division Commissioner for South-West Notts. 1928-35.

Minnie Trease (1879-1951)

Mary Isabel Trease (always known as Minnie) was born in Loughborough, one of eight children of George and Annie Trease. In 1897 her father took over Weavers Wine & Spirit Merchants and they moved to Nottingham, where the business is still run by the Trease family.

Minnie was an aunt of the author Geoffrey Trease, and he writes of her with great affection in the first volume of his memoirs, *A Whiff of Burnt Boats* (recently reissued):

> "There were three [aunts] – Ethel, Min and Daisy...
> Ethel, florid, sweet and gently dithery, had worked for some years as a governess and ranked as faintly bookish. Min was solid, blunt and a shade severe, impressive in her uniform as Captain of All Saints' Girl Guides. I once disgraced myself by referring to her as 'fat' and had to apologise abjectly for telling the obvious truth, no doubt a useful early warning for an embryo writer. Min was really a much-loved character, especially to the girls she devotedly took camping in Scotland every year. No working-class Guide, however poor, was denied that annual treat, whatever fund-raising efforts and face-saving subterfuges were called for in the preceding eleven months. Daisy, the youngest aunt, had shown artistic leanings and for a time attended the School of Art."

From 1917 – 1949 Minnie Trease was Captain of 11th Nottingham (All Saints) Company and her exceptional length of service is commemorated with this small plaque to the left of the altar in the church. She was also 11th Nottingham Ranger Captain until at least 1928 and from that date District Commissioner for Nottingham East District, Forest Division.

Minnie continued to live in the family home, 85 Waterloo Terrace, for many years with her sisters, Annie Esther (Ethel) and Edith Gertrude (Daisy). She was ready with good advice for her nephew after he won a scholarship to Oxford University:

> "The scholarship was all very fine, but as Auntie Minnie told me in her blunt, Girl Guide Captain way, I should not find it enough. I should need what she called 'parlour tricks'. She advised me, for a start, to take up tennis."

A Hundred Years Ago

In the Editiorial of the *Girl Guides' Gazette* for May 1925, the Chief Guide reflected on those early days of Guiding:

> "Those of you who have grown up with the Movement from its earliest days will look back to the years between 1909 and 1915 with a certain amused and half-regretful pride. They were indeed a body of plucky pioneers who 'did Guides' in the face of opposition, apathy, criticism and all manner of difficulties which, thanks to their work and the march of time, have now faded away into oblivion.
> And now ... we may indeed be proud and happy at all that has been accomplished; but coupled with these feelings is one which cannot be called 'content'. No. We must never rest content with ourselves or with what we are achieving."

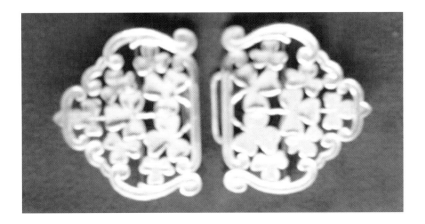

Above: Minnie Trease's silver trefoil belt buckle. Not standard issue, probably a presentation gift.

4. Early days

Agnes Baden-Powell (1858-1945)

Sir Robert Baden-Powell's elder sister Agnes was keenly interested in all he was doing with the Scout movement. In 1908 she began a Boy Scout troop herself and believed that girls should be able to enjoy the same opportunities as they did. After the events at Crystal Palace, Baden-Powell appealed to Agnes to help him form an organisation for girls and we can imagine that she leapt at the chance to do so.

Agnes was the ideal person to pioneer the Girl Guides. She was in many ways the product of a typical genteel Victorian upbringing: she was a fine amateur artist, she played the organ, piano and violin and was a member of Queen Mary's Needlework Guild. But Agnes also loved sport – cycling (including bicycle polo), swimming and skating – even hot-air ballooning! She was also passionately interested in natural history and the home she shared with her mother in London was literally alive with butterflies, small birds - and bees! The bees came in and out of the house by their own entrance and Agnes coaxed them into forming decorative honey-combs and harvested their prize-winning honey. "It is nice" she wrote, "to have pets that are tame and know you. I have had the dearest little sparrow for eleven years, who wears a tiny silver bell on a thread round his neck and flies after me wherever I go" (*How Girls Can Help* p 52). She was also familiar with 11 languages, and studied astronomy and science.

There were some 6,000 girls already registered when Agnes took charge of the new movement, and 1st Pickney's Green Company (the plucky Crystal Palace girls) had the honour of being known as "Miss Baden-Powell's Own". By 1915 the Girl Guides had official recognition and Agnes was made their President, an office she held until 1920 when she handed it over to Princess Mary, remaining Vice-president until her death in 1945 at the age of 86. Agnes was an extraordinary woman, a real "all-rounder" who was able to stand up to the inevitable prejudice against Guiding in the early days.

The Handbook for the Girl Guides or How Girls Can Help to Build Up the Empire

Agnes produced two pamphlets in 1909 to help the new movement on its way, but in 1912 this book was published, a re-worked version of *Scouting for Boys*, by Robert and Agnes Baden-Powell. It is generally referred to by its shortened title, *How Girls Can Help*. In her Introduction, Agnes declared the aim of Guides was to "get girls to learn how to be women – self-helpful, happy, prosperous, and capable of keeping good homes and of bringing up good children."

Ah, so that was it! Girls were the future mothers of the nation and should be properly trained for the purpose. The training was to be:

"...attractive to all classes, but more especially [to] the girls of the factories and of the alleys of our great cities, who, after they leave school, get no kind of restraining influence, and who, nevertheless, may be mothers.

Almost every man who rose to be a great man in history was helped largely by his mother... Britain has been made great by her great men, and these great men were made great by their mothers" (p 24).

Perhaps Agnes was thinking of her celebrated brother here? And, rather like the Girls' Evening Homes, "the Girl Guides system of training also gives a grand field for national work to young women who have had a better upbringing, but whose lives are at present largely wasted..." This was something that more fortunate girls could do for their disadvantaged sisters.

There was certainly a strategy for public acceptance in the tone of the book – if men and the Empire were to benefit, then girls must be allowed to do their bit – in fact it would be positively unpatriotic to forbid them, but always with this proviso –

"[W]e none of us like women who ape men... It is far finer to be a real girl... one [i.e. a man] loves a girl who is sweet and tender, and can gently soothe when wearied with pain." (p 22)

But, as she got further into the book, the eager girl 'Scout' would find much to absorb and excite her: life saving (from fire, water, trains, automobile accidents – the lot), first aid, woodcraft, camping (or campaigning, as it is described, in B-P's military tone) - all activities requiring strenuous exercise, team-work, physical endurance and discipline. "Fun" is not a word used much in this book, but great fun it must have been for these early Guides, tracking and 'spooring' in the woods, signalling, making camp-sites, cooking in the open and learning self-reliance. Guides, like Scouts, became a by-word for "Being Prepared" and knowing what to do in emergencies.

Small Brother (whose sisters are working for their Girl Guides' ambulance badge), "Come on, here's a bit of luck for you. I've made Rupert's nose bleed."   *Punch* May 20th 1914

It is also worth remembering that in the early 1900s many a young woman might consider emigration to Canada, America or Australia a good choice, and might, consequently, find herself in remote and hostile. places, where the practical skills of the Girl Guide could prove invaluable, maybe even the difference between life and death.

Courage and initiative were encouraged, and popular heroines like Nurse Craufurd of Mafeking, Florence Nightingale, Canadian patriot Laura Secord and Elizabeth of Hungary were held up as role-models, as well as many examples of ordinary girls and women who had saved lives and property by their courage and cool-headedness. However, girls and women of 1912 were still expected to behave pretty much as their Victorian mothers and aunts in the company of the opposite sex:
On Modesty:

> "Guides are modest in their behaviour. They go about their business or pleasure quietly and
> gently, and never draw attention to themselves unnecessarily by behaving noisily and talking
> or laughing loudly in public. They should be particularly careful of this when in the company of
> boys or men. Girls and boys should be comrades, so never do anything in word or deed to
> make a boy or man think less of you, and so lose his respect by making yourself cheap.

Remember familiarity breeds contempt. Don't romp about with a boy whom you wouldn't like your mother or father to see you with." (p 376)

On Humility:
"Humility, or being humble, was one of the things which was practised by the knights... although they were generally superior to other people in fighting or campaigning, they never allowed themselves to swagger about it. So don't swagger. And don't imagine you have got rights in this world except those that you earn for yourself... Do your duty first, and then you will earn your rights afterwards." (p 377)

Girls were expected to act like the "knights of old" but also to be "gentle and sweet, unselfish and true" and become the sort of woman a man "can place on that pedestal he has erected in his inner consciousness, and look up to as some one nobler and better than himself." To be worthy, a Guide must "understand men's requirements and tastes so as to be their comrades, but they must also maintain a refining influence and command their respect and their admiration." The expectation that girls were by nature nobler and finer beings than boys and must always exert a good influence over them was a hang-over from the Victorian Age; increased freedom through organisations such as the Guides could only, for the time being, at least, be enjoyed so long as girls remembered they were "ladies" and behave with refinement and modesty, because "one loves a girl who is sweet and tender."

In spite of all this, *How Girls Can Help* contains a section on careers for girls, not just as telephonists and shorthand typists, either, but in previously all-male professions like architecture and stock-broking. Women pioneers in various fields are cited as admirable role models, such as Elizabeth Blackwell and Mrs Garrett Anderson, two of the earliest Englishwomen to qualify as doctors, the famous scientist Marie Curie, and early women aviators. Guides were literally encouraged to aim for the skies. Girls with more modest aspirations were encouraged to earn money by things like keeping chickens, market gardening, carpentry and basket-making, because, "Guides never like to feel themselves indebted, and it is one of the laws of Guides not to beg."

How Girls Can Help was replaced in 1918 by a much more accessible handbook, *Girl Guiding* by Sir Robert Baden-Powell, himself.

5. What they wore

In the beginning there was no prescribed uniform. *How Girls Can Help* states, "Uniforms for Girl Guides are not compulsory," and devotes fewer than two pages to the subject. Although the bush-hats, tie and belt quickly became essentials, it was some time before Guides all wore regulation colours and clothing. Many Guides made their own uniforms and early Girl Guide novels describe the lengths they went to in order to be smartly turned out.

In *The Girl Scout* by Brenda Girvin (1913), believed to be the earliest example, Aggie and her five friends struggle to do things properly in order to emulate her brother, Peter's, Scout troop:

> "We must do the thing quite properly," said Ruth: "swear ourselves in, have a name, a uniform dress, and a call, known only to ourselves."
>
> "But I don't see how we can get a uniform?" Joan demurred. "I am sure that mother would object to buying Phyl and me new dresses."
>
> "As if anybody was going to have new dresses!" Aggie cried.
>
> "Our 'gym' tunics now," suggested Patty.
>
> "Oh yes," said Ruth, "they're brown, just the colour of the trees. They'll be grand."
>
> "And we'll wear our yellow dancing sashes," Patty cried, "fastened crossways over our shoulders."
>
> "We'll wear school satchels for haversacks," Aggie piped in quickly, "and we'll get garden sticks for staves; and because I'm leader I must have something special tied to my staff."

The "Spouts", as they call themselves, manage more by luck than judgement to solve a burglary and catch a gang of dangerous spies, outwitting the Scouts, and they receive their due reward:

> It was the Colonel himself who unpacked the parcel, and oh! What a long time Aggie thought he took to untie that string!
>
> Having untied the string the Colonel took off the lid; but even yet the contents were not revealed, for layer upon layer of tissue-paper had next to be removed.
>
> The girls edged nearer and nearer. Then the Colonel, smiling all the while, for he knew what pleasure he was about to give, drew out of the box five dark-blue skirts, five pale-blue jerseys, five red caps and five pale-blue neckerchiefs; five belts with pouches, and five haversacks. On each jersey was a shoulder knot of dark-green cashmere, and worked on each left breast was a sprig of laurel.
>
> "What – what does it all mean?" cried Aggie, her eyes fixed upon the wonders which lay spread on the table.
>
> She had not even dared to touch them with her fingers. Her comrades, too, could only look and marvel.

Illustration from *Terry the Girl Guide*

"It means," said the Colonel, "that some of the finest and bravest girls I know are to become members of that great body of Girl Guides which is being formed throughout the kingdom. Even as England has need of her men, so England has need of her women... You girls of today will be the women of the future, so you must learn to be the women of whom England will be proud."

But Aggie suddenly has a horrible thought:
"Why, there are only five skirts, five jerseys, five of everything! Which of us isn't to be a Girl Guide?"
But the Colonel only laughed.
"By the way," he turned to Aggie, "how old are you, young lady?"
"I shall be fourteen on Saturday," said Aggie proudly.
"Fourteen," repeated the Colonel. "Well, the Guides don't as a rule have their leaders under fifteen years of age, but we shall have to stretch a point this time."
And then from underneath yet another fold of tissue-paper he drew out a sixth uniform. On the left arm of the tunic were two white stripes.
"This uniform," he said, "is to be worn by the Leader of the 'Laurels,' as your Patrol is to be called for the future... A moment or two ago I said that you would have to look to your laurels. You have won them – won your Patrol, that is to say. Now you will have to look to them to see that you and they together win fresh laurels – win the finest laurels that England has to offer in future years."

In another early Guide story, *Terry the Girl Guide* by Dorothea Moore, Terry and her friends at the Manor School take tubs of khaki and blue "Dolly Dye" to their white school blouses and stockings in order to create their uniforms. The decidedly patchy results are, however, recognised for what they are intended to be when the girls go into the village shop:

"Deary me! It's the Girl-Guides come to visit us. Do you see, Thompson? Look at that now?"
Mrs Thompson cried delightedly.
Mr Thompson took his pipe out of his mouth and allowed that he saw.

In the first edition of this story the girls dyed their blouses khaki, but in later editions the colour was changed to blue, as Guide uniforms were regulated and other details added. Another notable change was that Terry's Bronze Cross for bravery was altered to The Nurse Cavell Badge which was introduced in 1919 in honour of Edith Cavell who was executed by the Germans in 1915.

Whilst uniform was not compulsory, *How Girls Can Help* does recommended that, "Guides should, as far as possible, dress alike, especially in each patrol, as regards hat, necktie, and colour of blouse." Certainly Guides would have wanted to be identified as such, and many new companies must have had to improvise. Agnes Baden-Powell wrote, "Girls should be encouraged to cut out and sew their own skirts and knickers (serge from 7d. upwards) also haversacks, stretcher-slings, flags, etc."

The distinctive accessories and shorter-than-usual skirts were soon familiar enough to attract adverse criticism in the press and rude remarks in the street. In 1912 the very first mention of the Guide movement in the *Southwell Diocesan Magazine* (which also covered Derbyshire) was a long letter of support from one "P.C.M." of Derby, extracts from which are reproduced below:

> "Everyone by this time is familiar with the sight of Boy Scouts going about the country in their picturesque garb, and most people know at least the outline of their training, and fully realize what a splendid organization it is. But comparatively few people have ever heard of the Girl Guides, and still fewer know anything about them, with the result that when a girl is seen wearing the Guide uniform people shake their heads and talk of the decadence of the nation, and consider it a sign of the times that girls should care to dress up in uniform and tear about the country like a lot of boys!

> "Alas, it is only too true that decadence is threatening the nation, the proofs are plentiful, and much of this is directly due to ignorance and supineness of our women. It was to check this growing evil that Miss Baden-Powell undertook to organize and start the Girl Guides, and put before girls of all classes, in an attractive way, pursuits which would enable them to become useful women and good mothers in the future.

> "The class of girls for whom this scheme is primarily intended are the girls who work in factories and workshops, and who spend the greater part of their spare time in the streets, without any aim or object, and with no restraining influence.

> "[W]e are often asked – "why is it necessary to be a Girl Guide to learn cookery, sewing, and all the rest? Don't girl's clubs and evening classes teach the same things?" The reply to the question is – certainly, the clubs do teach the same things as far as the actual handiworks go, and very splendid things they are too, but the Girl Guide training goes further than that, it deals also with the moral side of the girls' characters. The Guide Law alone shows us this, for are not the chief points of the Law to do with honour, loyalty, chivalry, unselfishness, gentleness, purity, cheerfulness, and the like. And above all it teaches them public spirit, and the honour and privilege of belonging to a body in which all are sisters working towards the same goal, and also working for the good of the whole.

> "[B]efore closing may I put a humble request to those who read this, that next time you meet a Girl Guide in uniform you will not say to yourself, "how absurd she looks, and how silly it is for girls to ape the Boy Scouts," but will sympathize and understand that there goes a girl who has a real honest desire to do her country a service by improving herself and helping her

fellow sisters to do the same, and who is ready to go through, and in most cases has to go through, the usual amount of jeering and sarcasm which the English public hurl at anything new or out of the common."

"P.C.M." sounds very much as if he/she was personally involved in Guiding in the Derby area.

EYEWITNESS: The day Captain's face turned blue!

"The first Guide company in Collingham was begun by Miss Aitcheson (Captain) and Miss Kitty Wigram (Lieutenant) and registered 16th September 1914, very soon after the beginning of the First World War. Early members were Dora Mathews, Florence Gould, Dora Burgess, Mary Maxwell, Elsie Kind, Elsie & Ada Armstrong, Aggie Drabble, Mary Hatcliffe, Nellie Russell.

An early photograph of 1ˢᵗ Collingham Co., undated

Meetings were held in the Rectory barn. They had camps – one at Barkwith, travelling from Collingham Station with Mr Kind, the station master in attendance. The first night a herd of pigs got into the field and Captain awoke to grunts and squeals – and shrieks from the Guides! It also rained so much they had to sleep in the hay loft of the farm. Another weekend camp was spent at Holme Hall. The carrier's cart was hired to take all the Guides while the Captain drove the gear in the dog cart. On the way it poured with rain and she had blue streaks down her face from the dye out of her hat! Uniforms were made of thick blue serge, with black stockings and shoes and a large navy felt hats were worn.

It is not certain when this company ceased, probably soon after the War, but the current company was registered 29th September 1927, and started by Miss Dorothy Browne (Captain) of Rutland House with Miss Dorothy Bradley of Winthorpe as Lieutenant. Some of the first

A Hundred Years Ago

Guides enrolled were Madge Linggard, Connie Osborne, Lily Revill, Clarice Haynes, Grace Morley, Jessie Wells, Cynthia Pratt and Marjorie Hatcliffe.

Meetings were held in Miss Browne's garden in the summer. It had a large lawn and a terrace where plays were often put on, a shrubbery and rough grass for stalking and tent-pitching, a pond, stream and trees of all kinds. What a grand place for the outdoor activities which made up the Guide programme!

1st Collingham Brownie Pack was formed in 1928 with Florence Gould as Brown Owl. Two older Guides, Cynthia Pratt and Marjorie Hatcliffe went round homes in the village recruiting and they soon had about thirty members. Many of the families could not afford uniforms, however, so a huge supply of scented cards was bought which they sold for one (old) penny each until all the Brownies had a uniform.

In 1932 a Ranger Company was formed with Captain Miss Nora Barber from Balderton. Some of the members were Win Bredwell, Margaret Green, Mary Akrill, Betty Tully, May Longford, Ross Ackrill and Dorothy Mosley. Miss Browne was Captain of the blind Rangers and she did a lot of work on Braille for them. They also camped with the Collingham Guides.

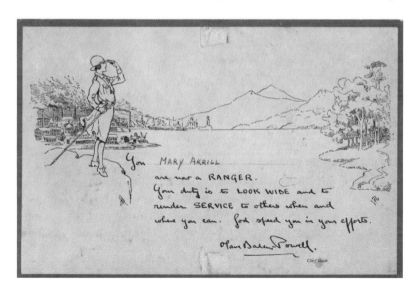

Mary Akrill was to become Captain in 1938 when Miss Browne retired, a position she held for thirty years. During this time the Guides did very well in Divisional events, Miss Akrill gave so much of her time to training the girls. She was awarded the Certificate of Merit for service to the movement."

[From an article by Miss J. M. Cubitt, courtesy Collingham & District Local History Society)

6. Brownies, too

Brownies are first mentioned in July 1914 in *The Girl Guides' Gazette* – though under a different name! They were formed as provision for all the younger girls aged 4 – 10 who longed to be Guides like their sisters but were not yet old enough. At first they were called "Rosebuds" but the name was so unpopular that by January 1915 the *Gazette* was canvassing its readers for something more suitable. Buds, Bees, Bantams and Skylarks were all names suggested, but in the end Baden-Powell himself came up with "Brownies", apparently inspired by a story by Juliana Horatia Ewing, written in 1865, which he probably remembered fondly from his own childhood.

The story features two lazy little boys, Johnnie and Tommy, who never do anything to help their father, a poor tailor. Their grandmother tells them about the Brownies – fairy-folk who used to do all the chores around the house while everyone was asleep. The lads think it would be a great idea to enlist a Brownie or two so they go and see the wise old Owl in the barn about it. The Owl explains to them that Brownies are really good children who help their parents without having to be asked. Idle, selfish children, on the other hand, are Boggarts and a curse to the house where they live. The boys take the hint and begin to get up early to light the fire and prepare breakfast so that their father doesn't have to waste time doing it, and gradually the family fortunes are reversed.

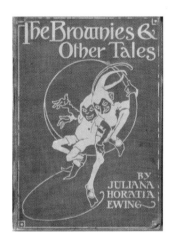

It's easy to see where the title Brown Owl came from, though it was three more years before a Warrant Standard was agreed for Brown Owls. Until then, the Brownie packs had often been large groups led by a young Guide, known as Mother Brownie, but this was regularised and "sixes" took over from large patrols.

The first Brownie Pack in Nottingham is thought to have been the one attached to 1st Nottingham (YWCA) Girl Guide Co., but many of the early Guide companies quickly formed Brownie packs too. The delightfully evocative photograph at the top of the page shows 44th Leenside Brownies in 1926.

Dresses which Brownies might wear. The first should be either brown or blue; the second and third blue; and the fourth brown. Nos. 3 and 4 are suggested as being the best.

The illustration above appeared in *The Girl Guides' Gazette*, December 1915. Brownies wore a blue uniform and pale-blue hair ribbons to begin with, but the familiar brown uniform gradually took over.

1st Nottingham (YWCA) Company with Brownies, 1917

7. The great and the good

The Chief Guide, Olave Baden-Powell (1889-1977)

As Chief Guide and then World Chief Guide for a total of nearly sixty years, Olave Baden-Powell was the internationally-recognised public face of the Girl Guide movement. It could be claimed that most of her long life was dedicated to Guiding. She had local connections and often visited Nottinghamshire in an official capacity.

She was born Olave St. Clair Soames on 22nd February 1889 at Stubbing Court, Wingerworth, near Chesterfield, the third child of Harold and Katharine Soames. The family business was brewing but Olave's father, who was an artist and poet of a somewhat restless disposition, soon sold the brewery, and throughout Olave's childhood they moved constantly from one country house to another, enjoying a comfortable life-style. Olave and her elder brother and sister, Arthur and Auriol, enjoyed the out-door life. Whilst living at Renishaw Hall, near Sheffield, they went boating on the lake and created their own secret society, and later, whilst living at Windermere, they sailed and had their lessons out of doors with a German governess. When Arthur was away at school, Auriol and Olave played happily together and put on concerts in the barn. Cycling (a new craze in the 1890s), tennis, squash, gymnastics and pony-riding were all taken up enthusiastically by Olave, in particular, but she never had any formal schooling, something which she always regretted. In her autobiography, *Window on My Heart*, she writes, frankly, "I was the dunce of the family."

In 1901, the family moved to Purley Hall in Berkshire to be close to London for 17 year-old Auriol's "coming out" into society, and here Olave found opportunities for rowing and canoeing on the River Thames. She enjoyed all kinds of sport and outdoor pursuits, which were to prove a good foundation for her later involvement in Guiding.

It is clear that she sometimes wondered what she would do with her "happy, sheltered, but utterly useless existence..." She was acutely aware that she "had no preparation for life at all" and longed to do something useful. She could not – and would not have been expected to – cook or sew, for example, and she was very aware that, had she belonged to a different social class, life would have been very different. It was expected, of course, that she would marry and have a family, but for the time being she preferred to accompany her father when he went shooting with the dogs and beaters. She also loved ratting, riding, cricket, swimming and fishing and by the time she "came out" herself in 1907, she admits that she was "still very much a tomboy." (*Window on My Heart*)

Olave's emergence was nowhere near as spectacular as Auriol's, though she had plenty of tennis partners and danced all night at hunt balls. She fell in and out of love and received several proposals of marriage, but it was not until she was travelling to Jamaica with her father on the RMS Arcadian, early in 1912, that she met the man whom she would marry and simultaneously discovered a sense of purpose for her life. The man was Sir Robert "Robin" Baden-Powell, hero of the Boer War and a bachelor more than twice her age. She called him "the Boy Scout man" and thought him modest and sweet. He saw in her, "honesty of purpose and common sense as well as a spirit of adventure." They fell in love, but as he was on his way to America and she to Jamaica, it was seven months before they met again. Needless to say, her family was not pleased: quite apart from the difference in age, Baden-Powell was relatively poor and had his mother and sister to support, while Olave was quite wealthy. Media interest in their unlikely romance was such that they had a very simple, quiet wedding.

Already interested in the Scouting movement, Olave began to accompany her husband to Scout rallies and on camping expeditions. During the First World War she learnt to drive and went to Calais with the Scouts to run a recreation hut for the troops – "I was doing a real job of work on my own," she wrote, triumphantly. She was, of course, aware of the emerging Guide movement, though at this stage it was still in the hands of her sister-in-law, Agnes. Olave offered her services in 1914 but was rebuffed (she and Agnes never really hit it off), but she persisted, and in March 1916 became County Commissioner for Sussex. She was made Chief Commissioner later that year.

In 1918, she became Chief Guide, a newly created post, though Agnes remained President until 1920 and then Vice-president until her death in 1945. The shy, uneducated girl was now full of confidence; she had found her purpose in life and was well-qualified for the job. Through the following years, she did everything she could to promote Guiding, travelling all over the world with her husband and sometimes deputising for him at Scouting events when he was unwell. In 1930 she was elected World Chief Guide, becoming a familiar figure and an inspiration to Guides everywhere. It is difficult to find a photograph in which Olave is not smiling – her cheerful, friendly, personality was legendary.

So far as Olave's connection with Nottingham goes, her mother's grandfather was Archdeacon Wilkins of Nottingham, and Katharine Soames often stayed at The Residence in Southwell as a child. In 1938 Lady Baden-Powell sent the Southwell Guides a curiously-carved wooden box (see left) which she said she had owned for 25 years and had been using for her letters. This box, which now resides safely in the archives at Girlguiding Nottinghamshire, was examined by experts last year when the Antiques Roadshow visited Southwell. It was decided that it was originally a prayer box, made from very ancient roof timbers removed during the restoration of Southwell Minster in 1844

Royal Approval

From its earliest days the Guide movement benefitted greatly from the interest and support of members of the Royal family, in particular Princess Louise and Princess Mary. Whatever misgivings people may have had about "girls in uniform", photographs of Royals in Girl Guide regalia must have gone a long way to convince them of its suitability for their own daughters.

Princess Louise (1848-1939)

In 1911, HRH Princess Louise graciously consented to become Patroness of the Girl Guides. The princess was the sixth child and fourth daughter of Queen Victoria, but had been cast in a different mould to her siblings. Louise had received a thorough education and was very artistic: she was a distinguished sculptor and artist, and a staunch supporter of women's suffrage. She did not enjoy life at court and was the only one of Queen Victoria's children to be allowed to marry a "commoner" – the Marquis of Lorne, heir to the Duke of Argyll. For some years her husband was Vice-Regent of Canada and so they lived abroad.

Princess Louise became involved with the Guides in the same year her husband's health began to decline (he died in 1914). No doubt her interest in education and self-determinism for women and girls attracted her to the emerging movement. She withdrew increasingly from the public eye after World War One, but she remained supportive of the Girl Guides until her death in 1939.

In a special message in *The Girl Guides' Gazette* in November 1917, during the War, she offered this piece of advice:

> "Train yourselves in the power of useful thinking, never act without thinking out what you are about to do and how you will do it. The habit of being methodical will then become second nature to you. It is a gift born with some and it is a valuable possession, but it can be acquired and should be encouraged since successful achievement depends so much upon it.
> "Good intentions are not enough, there must also be method in the carrying out of anything, and, to ensure success, there should be plenty of energy and determination too.
> "Don't worry to try to do what you feel you cannot do properly. Very few people have all-round powers...
> "Sympathy is one of the most important attributes for the Guides, as it leads in the right direction and is a source of endless helpfulness."

Princess Louise at a Rally in Chelmsford, 1920

Princess Mary (1897-1965)

Princess Mary was a great-granddaughter of Queen Victoria, daughter of the Duke and Duchess of York (later George V and Queen Mary). The Princess was educated at home, partly with her three brothers, and became a competent linguist. Her brother David (better known as Edward VIII) is reported as saying, "What a pity it's not Mary [who will be King]; she's far cleverer than I am." She remained very close to this brother after his abdication. She was not propelled into society as a girl; her father did not become King until she was 14 and she was able to enjoy as natural a childhood as possible. She was comfortable with all classes of people and able to speak to them with genuine interest and sympathy.

Although her coming-of-age in 1918 was very low-key, due to the War, she quickly began to assume public responsibilities and her war work alongside Queen Mary in municipal kitchens, visiting the wounded, rolling bandages, and helping in the canteen at a munitions factory, made her a popular Princess. She toured Voluntary Aid Detachments (VADs) and Queen Mary's Army Auxiliary Corps (QMAAC) camps in France and interested herself in the Red Cross, the National Organisation of Girl's Clubs and the Women's Land Army. She trained as a nurse at the Hospital for Sick Children in Great Ormond Street, entering as an ordinary probationer and receiving no different treatment to anybody else. She was known for her calmness and self-control in the medical and surgery wards.

It is hardly surprising that she was also interested in Guiding and by 1917 was President of the Norfolk Guides. On 4th November 1919, she appeared in front of 14,000 Guides at the Victory Rally at the Albert Hall in London in the uniform of a Guide Commissioner, and publicly allied herself with the Girl Guide movement. In the spring of 1920, HRH Princess Mary was enrolled by Lady Baden-Powell and became President of the Girl Guides, a position she held until her death in 1965. This was no nominal appointment; she always took a keen personal interest in Guiding and remained as involved as possible, expecting Lady Baden-Powell to keep her up to date with everything.

The Princess married Viscount Lascelles, eldest son of Lord Harewood, in 1922 and they made their home at Harewood House. As wedding presents, the Guides gave her, among other items, a diamond and ruby Tenderfoot brooch and two silver statuettes of a Guide and a Brownie. All the Guides in the Empire contributed, none being allowed to give more than one penny each.

Princess Mary in Nottingham

On 30th April 1927 Princess Mary came to Nottingham to open new extensions to Nottingham General Hospital and the Nottingham Children's Hospital and the Guides were out in force. Mansfield Guides lined the main road into town while other companies assembled on University Boulevard, and 500 Guides lined the Ropewalk. The City Commissioner's Minute Book states that the flags for the guard of honour at the hospital were to be the Union Jack of 1st Bottesford and the company colour of Nottingham's oldest city company, 1st Nottingham. All Guides taking part were to wear a pale blue tie and the Rangers a red one.

The Princess was accompanied by her husband Viscount Lascelles, the Duke and Duchess of Portland, the Marchioness of Tichfield and Lady Charles Bentinck, the Mayor and Mayoress and other civic dignitaries. Leaving Welbeck Abbey at 10am, she made stops, at Ellerslie House on Gregory Boulevard, the new University buildings and the War Memorial on Victoria Embankment. In a very full schedule, she then opened the new Co-operative Bakery on Meadow Lane, had lunch at the Guildhall, and finally arrived at the General Hospital at 2.45 pm to be greeted by Guides from the city and county of Nottingham. At the Children's Hospital Brownie Sixers were present, who were later treated to tea by Sir John Player. When the Royal party left town at 5pm, yet more Guides were stationed on the Mansfield Road to watch her go. It seems to have been a long and busy day, not only for Princess Mary, but for the many Guiders, Guides, and Brownies involved. The logistics of organising them all must have been extremely difficult, but it must also have been very exciting for the girls to have the opportunity of greeting their President.

A letter to Lady Readett-Bayley from the House Governor and Secretary of the General Hospital, M. MacColl, after the event reads, "I am desired to convey to you and those responsible for the Guard supplied by the Girl Guides, my Committee's warm appreciation of the part taken by them on the occasion."

Guides of 44th Nottm. (Leenside) Co. relaxing as they wait for Princess Mary

Other Royals who were to lend support to the Guide movement include HRH Princess Alice, a Vice-President of the Association 1931-1981, Lady Elizabeth Bowes-Lyon (the Queen Mother), who was District Commissioner for Glamis in 1921, our own Queen Elizabeth, her sister, the late Princess Margaret, and their daughters.

8. "Daughters of England" - the First World War

"When England, in peril, shall summon her sons,
The sword to unsheath, or to stand by the guns,
In service more gentle her daughters will share
Her burden of Empire, its sorrow and care"

(From a popular Guide song, *Daughters of England*, which was available from Girl Guide HQ for 3d.)

1914: The movement was relatively young when Britain was plunged into War in 1914, but all the evidence points to the Girl Guides rising to the occasion, putting some of their newly-acquired skills to good use and generally playing their part at a time of national crisis.

In March 1914, the newly-published *Girl Guides' Gazette* advised its readers to "Save your orange peel – dried orange peel makes excellent fire-lighters since it contains a highly flammable oil." Tips of this kind were to become essential over the next few years, though oranges were to become pretty scarce!

By the September issue the war was into its third month and there was a simple pattern for making "ration bags" for soldiers: the war effort had begun in earnest. Agnes Baden-Powell wrote:

"We are passing through a time of grave emergency... Guides should now be perfecting their Morse signalling... so as to be ready to telegraph when required. Fire-Rescue should also be practised, as Guides should all know where the hosepipe is kept, how to screw it on and turn the water on, as well as off, learn how to prevent the smoke choking you by wetting a stocking; also practise jumping from a height into a mat, and how to hold a mat tight and firmly between a dozen people.

"You all seem anxious to be helping, and there are many ways in which you can be of use in Soup Kitchens, or Day Nurseries, packing parcels and addressing them, as clerks, accountants, cyclists or interpreters."

She went on to mention the newly-formed Rosebuds (soon to be re-named Brownies). Even they, she suggested, could crochet woollen mittens and knit scarves for soldiers, roll bandages and collect magazines and books for invalids. She finished by reminding them all, "You who are at home are as much on duty as the men at war."

1915: Each month the *Gazette* reported what Guides were doing around the country and these reports, sent in by the companies themselves, are an indication of what Nottinghamshire was doing to help the War effort. For example, in April 1915, the Hucknall Torkard Company, who had only recently had their Company Colours dedicated at the Parish Church, had completed a number of 'hussifs' containing useful articles for the soldiers at the Front, and scarves for Scouts on coastguard duty.

A War Service Badge was soon announced for all Guides and Guide Officers who, by the end of the War had performed:

> Not fewer than twenty-one days' special service for Hospitals, Nursing Institutions and other Public Departments or Societies or Girl Guide Hostels. This service must be at the request of some competent authority, and must be carried out for at least three hours per day.

> Not fewer than 15 articles personally-made, to include 4 pairs of socks, 4 pairs of mittens, 2 shirts, 1 pyjama suit, 1 child's garment, 1 woman's garment, 1 belt, and 1 bed-jacket. Knitting and needlework already done for Sailors, Soldiers, Sea Scouts, Belgian Refugees, Hospitals, etc., may count.

> For twenty-one days' work, not necessarily consecutive, for paid employment in connection with recognised firms working directly for the Government in connection with the War, or in connection with War Service for Women initiated by the Government Labour Exchanges. In such work for instance as Farm Work, Dairy Work, Market Gardening, Poultry Farming, Light Machining for Armaments, Clothing Machining, Brush Making etc., etc.

In the same issue, Lt.-Gen. Sir Robert Baden-Powell, under the extraordinary heading, "The Zeppelins are coming, Hurrah! Hurrah!" exhorted the Guides to Be Prepared to give valuable first-aid to their fellow townspeople in the event of air raids. He also suggested they get up concerts and other free entertainments in their club rooms and the set up Invalid Kitchens and Day Nurseries.

> *Girl Guides' Gazette* **Feb. 1915**
> A new use for stocking tops – making cosy warm jumpers for little children. When the worn parts, the foot and heel have been cut off, the tops of golfers' and shooter's stockings [socks] are joined together length-wise, and two more are used for the sleeves.

1916: 3rd Nottm. (YWCA), a company barely a year old, reported it had already gained four War Service Badges and a War Savings Association had been formed for members. (*Girl Guides' Gazette* Aug. 1916).

A Home-grown Heroine: Zillah Butler

On August 31st 1916, one Nottingham Girl Guide became a real heroine: 15 year-old Zillah Butler of the 1st Nottm. (YWCA) Co. plunged into the River Trent to save a five-year-old boy from drowning. Using her life-saving training she pushed through the helpless crowd, leapt into the river and managed to bring the boy ashore. She then modestly slipped away, caught a bus and went home to Carrington. Fortunately, she was followed by a man who had witnessed her bravery, and he informed the police of where she lived. Lord Baden-Powell subsequently presented Zillah with her Life Saving medal. She went on to become the first Guide in Nottingham to win her Gold Cords in 1921 and was Lieutenant of 1st Nottm. (YWCA) Company 1921-24 before becoming Captain of the 1st Arnold Company in 1924. In 1926 she married Henry Munson and joined him first in missionary work in West Africa and later as a Seventh-Day Adventist Minister in Chester. She died in 1995.

Zillah Butler receives her medal from Baden-Powell

Guides pass muster

On September 9th 1916 Baden-Powell visited Nottingham to inspect Scouts and at his request about 150 Guides were also present. The Chief Scout expressed his pleasure at seeing so many badges for proficiency in homecraft, and also those earned for public service during the War. This was the first time the Nottingham and Notts. Girl Guides had paraded and the review was "a great success... The fact that the Guides were inspected and addressed by Sir Robert Baden-Powell will make the day a memorable one for all." (*Girl Guides' Gazette* Oct. 1916)

1917: 1st Collingham, who took part in the above review, had by May 1917 gained 11 War Service Badges and seven "very keen" Guides had passed the Nursing Test, the Quartermaster at the local VAD Hospital being very much pleased with the work. Patrol Leader Dora Matthews had also rendered valuable assistance pumping water at a haystack fire the previous July.

The Duchess of Portland, County President, inspected seven registered companies in Nottingham on May 12th and warmly congratulated the girls on their efficiency. The companies competed in laundry, cooking, needlework, bedmaking, bandaging, knitting, singing, drawing and flagmaking. 3rd (Castle Gate) Company won 1st prize, with 2nd prize going to 1st Nottm. (YWCA).

How Guides helped

Miss Baden-Powell, in the face of food-shortages, urged all Guides to grow vegetables in any spare bit of ground they could find, even in London where, "I have even seen a row of pots on a window-sill growing fine lettuces. At Buckingham Palace the King has had potatoes planted in all the flower beds."

There was certainly plenty that a Guide could do, what with life-saving, signalling, collecting sphagnum moss for dressing wounds, agricultural work, war savings and putting on patriotic displays. Country Guides were requested to collect sheep's wool off hedges to send to the Wool Depot to make blankets for soldiers, and to harvest 'weeds' such as groundsel, thistles, dandelions and foxglove leaves for the Vegetable Drug Co. Nothing was wasted.

Another War Service Badge was announced which could be earned for 100 hours work in any garden or allotment or on the land, which may help to increase the food of the nation, for which the Guide must receive no wage nor be in direct receipt of profits from produce sold.

Guides raised funds for the French recreation huts manned by Olave Baden-Powell and her colleagues, and Lady Readett-Bayley was driving ambulances to the front line. Both provided strong role-models. The War must actually have been a wonderful opportunity for girls to attempt all kinds of things they had never done before, with the very good excuse that they were supporting the war effort.

Nottingham Patrol Leader off to France

An interesting gathering was held at the YWCA, Shakespeare St., Nottingham, to wish God-speed to Miss Phoebe Brittan a Patrol Leader of the 1st Nottm. Girl Guides and also a member of the YWCA, who is going to France on war work. Miss Andrews (Captain) on behalf of the company, presented her with a handsome Red Cross first-aid case, beautifully lined with every requisite. Miss Andrews said it was with the deepest regret that they were parting with Miss Brittan who had been a splendid worker, but they were proud to think of the sacrifice she was making, giving up everything to go to France, and they sincerely hoped to have her back with them after the War. Miss Brittan was the recipient of a travelling rug from Miss Andrews and many other useful presents from members of the YWCA.
(*Our Outlook*, March 1918)

1918 saw the introduction of Nottinghamshire's own County Badge, depicting a brass hunting horn, similar to that of the Sherwood Foresters.

1918: Lady Baden-Powell at Mansfield

The Chief Guide visited Mansfield in June 1918 to inspect the Mansfield and Kirkby Guides at the Girls' Club, Chesterfield Road. As well as the Guides, many local dignitaries were present, including the Mayor and Mayoress, to welcome Lady Baden-Powell and Lady Seely, the County Commissioner. The festive occasion was obviously appreciated by everyone as a welcome diversion during those final months of World War One.

Lady Baden-Powell addressed the three companies of Guides present and her remarks indicate some of the ways Guides were contributing to the War Effort:
People in Mansfield, she said, would be watching them and would be asking what these Girl Guides were doing. They did many things that were useful, in fact there was a good motive behind all that they were taught. She hoped that they would make themselves efficient with their ambulance work and ever be ready to render assistance. They did not want to go about hunting for accidents, but they ought to be ready for any emergency. Then again, they were taught to be thrifty in their clothes. Their uniform stood for service – service for someone else. The Girl Guides movement was not a recruiting ground for the WAACs [Women's Auxiliary Army Corps]. All the same they were doing something for their country.... The next time she came she hoped they would have learned a little more about service and the objects generally of the movement and that they would have increased their efficiency. "It is jolly important you should know how to use a bandage, for you never know what may come your way." There were many ways in which the Guides could be useful. In addition to the collection of waste paper, now so valuable, they could gather eggs for the wounded, work in canteens, etc., and they must always be ready to lend a hand, "Be prepared to live up to your motto, girls, and the great big splendid Guide laws. Remember your promise when you joined to honour God and the King. Do a good turn whenever you can, behave yourselves, be smart in all you do, if you are neat in your dress you will be neat in other things. Good luck to you all. The Girl Guides' game is one worth playing..."

She went on to address the parents present, assuring them that a Guide training would prepare their daughters for a useful future when the War was over.

The Mayor, in proposing a vote of thanks, remarked how glad he was to hear how the movement trained the girls bodily, mentally, and, above all, spiritually. It was a splendid organisation, and the visit of Lady Baden-Powell would, he was sure, create a good deal of enthusiasm for it in Mansfield. Local clergy added their warm support; the Chief Guide had done much to convince the town that Girl Guides were a good thing.

(From a much longer article in the *Mansfield & North Notts. Advertiser*, 21st June 1918)

Wanted!

By end of the War, Guides were in demand for paid work because they had earned a reputation for acting conscientiously, using their initiative and shouldering responsibility.

The April 1915 *Gazette* states. "Guides have made such a good name for themselves that many people are anxious to employ them - in fact, the demand is greater than the supply."

In November 1918 there appears an advertisement for Guides aged 14 and over to work in Government Offices as messengers for 12s 6d a week plus meals; and all kinds of posts were regularly advertised for girls and young women who were Guides or Rangers on the premise that their Guide allegiance was proof enough of their abilities.

In Mrs Hann's story, *Smiler, a Girl Guide* (1925), fourteen-year-old Gwendolen "Smiler" Moran, gains a post in a prestigious West End store when her Captain advises her to wear her Guide Badge at the interview. "I see you're a Guide," her interviewer observes, "that goes a long way with me."

In the aftermath of the Armistice, Guides were reminded:

> "The years of war have brought great changes to the women of England. They have brought even greater responsibilities. It is for us now to reap where others have sown; but it may never be forgotten that others will reap our sowing. Let us face the future, realising all that it holds, and the solemn hour that is ours today, and let us "make good."

(Written by Miss Muriel Messel, County Secretary of Sussex, just before her death in the Influenza epidemic, and published in the *Gazette*, December 1918.)

9. The 'Twenties

After the War, life gradually began to return to something like normal and companies of Brownies, Guides and Rangers multiplied throughout the county. In 1921 there were 17 Companies with 1796 Guides 643 Brownies and 48 Rangers led by 168 Guiders. Companies were often run by clergy wives, sisters and daughters, and in small towns and villages they provided a happy, useful outlet for local girls, as Dorothy Smith's experience relates:

EYEWITNESS: Dorothy Smith (1901–2003)
Born in Ordsall, where her father was curate, Dorothy attended St Elphin's School for the daughters of the clergy in Darley Dale, where she became head girl. The family moved to Cuckney when her father became vicar there, and then to St Wilfred's, Kirkby in Ashfield.

> "In the February of 1920 we moved to Kirkby. That was one of the loveliest summers of the century. We found when we got there that they had a quite small, but quite flourishing little Guide company. It had been started by the curate's wife and they had moved to Liverpool, and the two girls who were keeping it going said to my father, "Is Miss Smith interested in Guides?" "Oh yes," he said!
> I didn't know very much about it when I started but you could get lots of training, you know. Another more experienced Guider would invite you to go and view her company, and every year we used to have a week's training for Guiders in the district.
> "We didn't go camping when we were in Kirkby because in those days, you know, the pits were working very badly and some of the fathers only worked two shifts a week. There wasn't much money and so we used to camp in the rectory orchard and cook our camp dinner and tea out there and they used to do all the different jobs round the camp site with their patrols. One patrol would go and do the shopping and it was a great thing to be the cook patrol of course. And then another patrol used to call themselves the Orderlies and the job they liked to do was to rake the paths around the rectory garden. Yes, and we had two or three bird baths in the garden and they used to like to go and take water for the birds. So they got all the camping experience and went home at night. Then on Sunday we used to plan a meal that would cook quickly and we used to go to church then they used to come down to get Sunday dinner ready. The congregation used to come and see what we were doing. It couldn't have been easier, and attached to the Rectory was a large Parish Room which we could use if it rained, we could all pile in there. I remember one of the mothers saying to me afterwards, "You know, it did Brenda as much good as a week at the seaside."

After her father died in 1937, Dorothy and her mother moved to Mapperley and joined the new St James Church, Porchester, where Dorothy taught Sunday School and ran Guides and Rangers. She was also Guide Commissioner for many years. After the death of her mother, she moved to Hazel Grove where she would host Summer Guide Meetings in her garden. 40 years after she left Kirkby her old Guides and Rangers were still visiting. She died just short of her 102nd birthday.

Dorothy Smith with 10 fellow-Guides from St Wilfred's Rangers at their 50th Reunion, 1988

Throughout the 1920s information about the doings of Notts. companies continued to be published in *The Guide* and *The Girl Guides' Gazette*. The *Gazette* was aimed more at Guiders and changed name in 1928 to *The Guider*.

March 1922:
Miss Agnes Boden, won a Trek-Wagon on behalf of 2nd Nottingham Co. by collecting "several hundred" coupons from *The Guide* magazine. The competition was so popular, *The Guide* offered another one and Nottingham triumphed again! The winner was Miss D. H. Gem of Nottingham Forest District, having collected 1,678 coupons!

  The Editor commented, "I don't know how they do it but they must have worked jolly hard."
The above photo shows 17th Nottm. Co. with a similar wagon in 1934.

1922: 3rd Nottingham (Castle Gate) Co. sent in reports of two contrasting camps at Aslockton in June and August!

"June 3 dawned at last, and a very happy Company set off to camp at Aslockton, a pretty little village in Nottinghamshire. The week was a very happy one from beginning to end, and will live in the memory of every Guide who went. All returned home looking very brown and well. Our Company will be seven years old soon, and we are looking forward to our birthday celebrations with gladness and with thankful hearts for all the blessings we have received during the past years."

However...

"The camps of the 3rd Nottingham are no ordinary affairs, and last August Bank Holiday week-end camp, spent at Aslockton, Notts., proved to be one of the most exciting we have ever had. Saturday and Sunday were glorious days and the sunshine was enjoyed to the full. The rain simply poured down on Monday and made it quite impossible for us to go out. We were far from dull, however, as the hall in which we slept made a splendid football ground; and in the evening we had a fancy dress dance followed by charades. When we awoke next morning we were surrounded by water. The fields at the back of us were converted into a very beautiful lake, and the road looked just like a river. We were obliged to paddle to the village, much to our enjoyment, and were only prevented from paddling to the station on our way home through the kindness of a farmer, who conveyed us to the station in a high trap. Naturally, almost the whole of Tuesday was spent by or in the water, as the sun shone brightly nearly all day. Some of us had great fun with a raft, while others contented themselves by simply paddling. Luckily, our camp itself stood on a mound and was kept quite dry; and we almost imagined that we were camping in Venice."

3rd Nottingham at camp, Woodhouse Eves, 1924, Sylvia Reddish centre

48

It was a wet summer all round:

> "The **2nd Mansfield** spent their fifth summer camp at Rowsley this year. Their camp was under canvas, but a terrible rainstorm in the "wee small hours" of their second day made it necessary to quit the tents and seek refuge in the spacious barns. They soon made themselves "comfy" here and the cooks set to work. Outings consisted of a trip to Haddon Hall, a charabanc ride, and a visit to Chatsworth House, and (by kind permission of the Duchess of Devonshire) we were conducted through all the beautiful rooms there, a day at Matlock, and an invitation to tea from the Nottingham Guides who were camping near by."(*The Guide* Nov. 18)

> "**16th Nottingham (St Christopher's)** – During August forty of us spent a very enjoyable week at Southwell, where we had the use of a cottage and schoolroom. On Sunday morning we attended service at the Cathedral, and on Thursday, the only really fine day, we were entertained by Lady Hicking at Brackenhurst Hall. On Friday, Archdeacon Conybeare took us on a very interesting tour over the Cathedral. We all enjoyed the climb to the top of the tower, and, even more, the visit to the belfry, where we saw the great hammers strike the hour. We were all sorry to return home, as we felt that our camp had been one of the jolliest weeks we have ever had together." (*The Guide* Dec. 23)

What is striking, is that these Guides were determined to enjoy themselves - whatever the weather!

"Don'ts" for Campers

➢ Don't construct the Patrol washhouse after dusk. It is apt to be less sufficiently screened than one imagines when viewed by the broad light of day.

➢ Don't make a pet of the camp cat. A wet furry animal is not the most congenial sleeping companion on a pouring wet night.

➢ Don't allow stray sheep within the camp boundaries. They are inclined to become a nuisance, and jump over the dinner table.

➢ Don't go to camp without your Guide smile. You will need it on your orderly day, when washing-up in the pouring rain, getting wetter ad wetter every minute; and washing under the same trying conditions in the early morning.
(*The Guide*, July 29 1922)

1923: Grave concerns

In the August *Gazette* "An Elderly Commissioner" was worried that Guide Camps were altogether too strenuous for girls. She also expressed her opinions on "midnight feasts":-

"I am sorry to say that in some camps the school custom of a "last night feast" has crept in, generally in tents at the last thing at night. This from two points of view is, I think, bad; first, if a Guide over-eats herself (and they easily can, especially if tired or excited) her mother has all the bother of her next day when she returns home, and probably blames camp-life generally, and not the feast! Also in Guiding we do want to take our Guides up to a higher level, and to show them that pleasures are not only gratifications of the appetites..."

1925: Smoke signals

A heated discussion ensued at Ranger Conference that year as to whether Rangers should be allowed to smoke at camp. One Ranger, who admitted to being a heavy smoker, thought it would be a bad example to Guides, especially because "a Guide is thrifty" and smoking an extravagance! Another Ranger thought smoking less detrimental than the excessive sweet-eating she had witnessed in camp (see advert on right!).

  In the end, the vote was for a complete smoking ban at Ranger camps.

(*Girl Guides' Gazette* Jan. 1925)

Fashions change!

In 1925, there was an urgent appeal for ideas to keep Guide hats secure on 'shingled' hair – a sign of the times! Many girls were shedding their long tresses and sporting close cuts (known as shingles) and were, in consequence, having trouble keeping their hats on!

  Such issues were bound to arise from time to time, and in 1928, a correspondent to *The Guider* ventured to enquire if there could be anything "immoral or vulgar" for uniform collars to be worn a little lower than previously, as fashions had changed so radically and these "uncomfortable, unhealthy chokers" were now antiquated and impractical. This letter invoked several more pleas, not just for looser collars, but for more comfortable uniforms altogether. There was also a real need for more informal attire for camping, including even, possibly, dispensing with ties and stockings! Headquarters responded promptly with the introduction of an overall-style uniform which allowed more freedom of movement and was cheaper to make or buy.

Skirts were worn much shorter now, as well, which was seen as no bad thing, as it enabled girls to run and swim and climb freely, but –

> "There is just a slight danger, though, that in this as in other new found liberties, we shall not quite know when to stop, and it behoves us Guiders to beware. With the very small Guides what follows does not concern, but there does come a time when discretion should be shown. The thighs of a big girl are not very attractive when seen, as they sometimes are, bulging out of tightly pulled-up knickers." (*The Guider* April 1929)

Girl Guides in demand

Employers continued to seek Guides and Rangers for various posts through the columns of *The Gazette*:

REQUIRED, secretary-chauffeuse, Fiat (new) car, to do running repairs; resident. Apply in writing, Girl Guide Headquarters, 25 Buckingham Palace Road, S.W.1 (*Gazette*, April 1925)

WANTED for East End Settlement, a well-educated girl with knowledge for Guiding. Salary. (*Gazette*, April 1925)

GOVERNESS wanted; January; Commissioner's 3 children; P.N.E.U. method essential; age over 25, under 40; willing to Captain Guide Company and Brownies. (*Gazette*, Jan 1926)

GENERAL MAID, small labour-saving cottage; good wages; bonus every six months; Ranger preferred. (*Gazette*, April 1926)

A letter in July 1926, requested a dedicated employment column as the writer had obtained better results from the *Gazette* than from anywhere else. This suggestion was immediately taken up and advertisements split into Domestic, Guiding and Educational. It has to be said, though, that some employers expected a great deal from applicants!

All sorts of other intriguing requests appeared in the *Girl Guides' Gazette*. In February 1925 there was an appeal for "dead animals in good condition" for stuffing for the museum cases at Foxlease. BUT "No creature must on any account be killed for the purpose of the collection"!

1926: At the end of 1926 the old Company Notes column in *The Guide* changed from routine reports of company doings to publishing only select reports of "amusing and interesting" items that might be of use to other companies. The Halloween party held by Mansfield and District Girl Guides was the first item to be published under this new description. The Guiders involved certainly appear to have gone to an incredible amount of trouble to ensure a memorable evening.

1926: Mansfield District Girl Guides' Halloween Party

"On the evening of Oct. 29th 300 Guides and Guiders of the Mansfield District met in a suitably decorated school, and lived for two hours in a story; all the Guides wore masks and Guiders were dressed as witches; the Divisional Commissioner appeared as a seventeenth century gentleman. Here is the story:

It was a dark, dark Halloween; all the old witches in the ancient town of Mansfield were gathered together in a secret chamber of the Witches' Palace. The young witches living in the district were assembled in the great hall, talking in groups of the coming events, when into their midst appeared the Ceremonial Witch. She blew a piercing note upon her whistle; the moments that followed were filled with expectation not unmixed with awe. A slight movement in one corner of the hall caused all eyes to be turned towards it, and slowly there came into the middle of the hall a procession formed by the "Storyland" Witches. Cinderella's godmother looked wonderfully fit, considering her great age. All the young witches gasped. Music filled the air as one and all joined in a merry ring. Suddenly the music stopped and shrieks took its place for the "Storyland" Witches were rushing hither and thither capturing and carrying off those of their choice. When all had been thus carried off to various chambers, music again filled the air, and sets for country dancing were formed by those who were under the "Dancers" spell. (The dancing and games were continuous.)

As the evening wore away, chamber doors were opened, and whispers of secrets were heard; black-cat magic was distributed; the candle-blowing power of some of the young witches was spoken of as "great." Some tried to blow the walls away in their efforts to blow out the flame; the Witch of Light blindfolded them first, you see. Wet locks and red noses told their own tale of water tubs and apples. Peals of laughter coming through one open door drew an eager crowd, and apples were found to be bobbing about on cords in front of mouths of all shapes and sizes. Some of the oldest and most serious of the young witches caused much merriment by their attempts to catch the bobbing things with their teeth. Cinderella's godmother was found to be in possession of a number of enchanted frogs who said "Um! Um!" and claimed young witches, as partners, in leaping races. The winning pair were given dainty tit-bits to feed upon.

At last when everyone had feasted upon apples and nuts, the brilliant light went out, and the soft light of the Ceremonial Witch's fire (over which hung a cauldron) and that of a hundred

weird smiling Jack-o-lanterns took its place. Rounds and songs were sung and everybody was under the spell of night when a visitor was announced. "It" (the visitor) proved to be a gentleman of the old days. "It" sat by the fire smoking its long pipe and telling tales of the "bad times, in the good old days." After "Its" departure a Derby Witch told the story of "Picalo," who found out it was the little things in life that count. Songs and stories finished, the "Ceremonial Witch" stirred the contents of her cauldron, and gave to each company of young witches a slip of paper with magic advice for the future written thereon; everyone scanned the slips eagerly and laughed at what they saw, and then – "Taps." And after, three rousing cheers for the old Witches.

This is a true story of what happened at the party."
(*The Gu*ide, Dec 18th 1926)

1927: Scouts and Guides

In 1927, Sir Montagu Burrows, Boy Scout County Commissioner for Oxfordshire, expressed his surprise that there was not closer co-operation between Scouts and Guides, noting that, "Scouts owe a great deal more to the help of ladies than Guides do to the help of gentlemen... a very large proportion of our best Cubmasters and Cub Commissioners are ladies, and I know some very excellent lady Scoutmasters."

This was very true. In the influential *Girl's Own Paper*, for example, which steadfastly ignored Guiding until at least 1927, girls were, however, encouraged to become Cubmasters *(sic)*, presumably because this was seen as a more "motherly" and "womanly" role, caring for small children? Incidentally, when the *GOP* did deign to notice Guiding, it was largely as a recommended occupation for unmarried women! –

> "Not only with regard to children can the unmarried woman give her inestimable help, but in all sorts of work for girls. The Girl Guide movement has tremendous potentialities of influence. I have observed," wrote Lily Watson, "that when women who have little prospect before them of marriage take up this work, it appears to fascinate and absorb them, and to fill up their life in a wonderful way..."   (*GOP* Vol. 48, 1927 p530)

It is certainly true that many Guiders *were* unmarried women – especially after WW1 when a huge number of young men had been killed – but it was by no means the norm! On the other hand, many women were discovering meaningful lives, careers and occupations that did not depend on marriage and motherhood and many dedicated their leisure time to Guiding.

To return to Sir Montagu Burrows – he believed the Scouts owed a debt to the Guides and suggested better communication between the two. He also noted that Guides had overtaken Scouts in some areas of inclusion e.g. with disabled girls and those living long-term in institutions. But there was always the issue of *just how much* mingling should be allowed between older boys and girls:

> "We have heard a great deal about "girlitis" in the Scout Movement, and surely one of the best remedies for the less desirable aspects of that complaint would be to introduce the adult Boy Scout to the adult Girl Guide; and this would be one of the natural results of co-operative efforts, whether camp-fires or entertainments. Of course there are limitations to be observed, and equally of course there are many prejudices to be overcome. All I want to suggest is a trial of the experiment."   (*Gazette*, 1927 p9)

1928: Lady Readett-Bayley offered to provide a County Standard and the design was discussed at the January Commissioners' Meeting. It is not known what happened to this first standard, the current one having been dedicated in 1951.

"Making Little Girls into Soldiers"

In *The Guider*, July 1928, the Chief Scout answered allegations of militarism made by "A Guider" in the *Evening Standard*. The writer's objection was that Guides had now become, "Over-Officered,

Over-drilled and Over-organised," and so super-efficient and regimented that all the fun had gone out of the movement.

> "The whole crux of the Guide business is very much the problem of the Scout business. It needs imagination, not routine. It needs sympathy, not discipline. The worth-while discipline has got to come from within the child. The kind you can enforce will slip off and be lost at the very age when it ought to be influencing the young character....
>
> "The Guider should be a big sister, friendly and jolly, putting aside the dignity of her years and just 'playing properly' in a delightful game with the younger people.
>
> "Given the right spirit though the whole thing, the children will respond with a self-taught respect and obedience... and their own sense of "playing the game" will bring out an order worth having."

The Chief answered in both the *Evening Standard* and *The Guider*:

> "We are not out to make soldiers of the girls... Guiding is not a formal course of instruction with rigid standards of attainment. It is a game, a comradeship of fun and laughter through which, under the capable inspiration of the elder sister, the girl emerges a happy, healthy and helpful citizen."

But, he concludes, "Anyhow, criticism is always good for us... it gives us warnings of which we should do well to take heed."

Women were still expected to be the "civilising sex", though. At The Imperial Camp at Foxlease, in July 1928, The Chief Scout, speaking on "The Value of Womanliness", whilst acknowledging women's many achievements in medicine, the arts education, government and politics (which must only be pursued for the common good, not selfish aims!), was still promoting stereotypes:

> "Women have the advantage over men in that they are individually and personally less selfish. If they can pass on that unselfish character to their menkind, to their sons and their husbands, they will be doing a service to humanity.
>
> "Nature gave to men the qualities of aggressiveness and pugnaciousness for selfish ends; while she gave women patience and peaceful instincts.
>
> "Herein lies another reason why we should encourage womanliness in the coming generation in opposition to the too frequent imitation of manliness."
> (*The Guider*, Sept. 1928)

These mixed messages were to continue for some years.

10th July 1928: Opening of Nottingham University – Another high-profile public event at which there were many companies of Guides and Scouts present. **Margaret Cooper** was in the Guard of Honour and says they were in an excellent position to have a good view of the King and Queen. *The Daily Guardian* noted, "From the East Court two lines of sombre blue made by 1,800 Girl Guides ran down to the gates, where the 45th & 1st Jewish troops of Scouts were stationed."

March 1929:

"Nottingham Guides ... are to be congratulated on their splendid muster for the parade of the Forest Division at St Mary's Church. Over 1,000 Guides took part in this. Two words coined by the Chief Scout, "Stickability" and "Happyfying," were used by Canon Gordon in his sermon. In a subsequent letter to the Press he wrote, "The work of Sir Robert Baden-Powell, who has taught to boys and girls the jolliness of responsibility and reliability (stickability) and the tremendous fun of helping other people (happyfying), will, I believe, endure longer and have more lasting influence than the most conscientious efforts of law makers and more pompous pedagogues." (*The Guider* March 1929)

Canon Gordon's wife, Mrs J. G. Gordon, had recently been appointed Division Commissioner to Forest Division. The same month, Mrs Gem, who had recently retired from that post, was presented with the Medal of Merit for "Good service to the movement."

Lady Baden-Powell at Ruddington, 29th June 1929

4,500 Guides greeted Lady Baden-Powell, who had stepped down as Chief Commissioner in 1926, at Ruddington Grange on 29th June 1929. The Chief Guide was accompanied by County Commissioner Lady Readett-Bayley and Division Commissioners Lady Maud Rolleston, Lady Phyllis MacRae, Mrs Dowson, Mrs Gordon, Miss Parker, Mrs Conybeare and Mrs Buxton. The march-past was "a most imposing spectacle" consisting of South-West, South, Forest, Plains, Newark, Southwell, Retford, Worksop and Mansfield divisions.

"Addressing the assembled guides, Lady Baden-Powell spoke of the delight it gave her again to come to Nottinghamshire. But at the time she had never contemplated seeing so fine a body of guides as that she had inspected that day. The way they had carried out the programme was a credit to their officers and themselves and she would carry away with her a very happy impression and recollection of what she had seen.

They were making themselves capable and helpful, able to do their own cooking, and taught to take the rough with the smooth.

This was an important year in the Girl Guide's history, for whilst their brother scouts were to hold their great jamboree they themselves were to form their own separate organisation and headquarters. There were now 100,000 more girl guides than boy scouts in the world. (Applause.) Towards the cost of their new headquarters she had received donations from the Gold Coast, India, Canada, New Zealand, and other parts of the world. She asked them to take, as their motto, "My country is a fine one, but I am going to do all I can to make it better still" (Applause.)

On the call of Lady Readett-Bayley, lusty cheers were raised for Lady Baden-Powell, and the County Commissioner was also similarly honoured.

The guides then filed past and offered their contributions to the Girl Guides' House Fund."
(From an unidentified newspaper article in Lady Readett-Bayley's album)

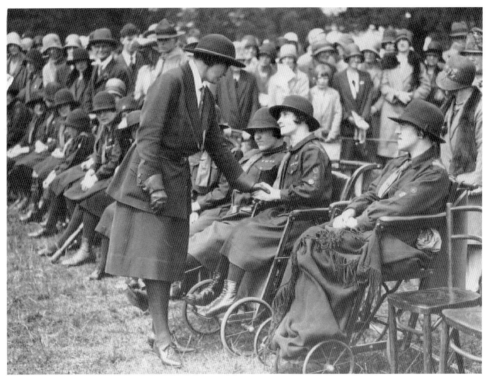

Lady Baden-Powell with Post Guides at Ruddington Grange, 1929

The march past at Ruddington, 1929

10. A camp of their own - Elton

As we have already seen, camping was a key activity for early Guides and Guiders. For urban Guides, a trip to the countryside must have been a great adventure – and maybe a bit scary! Though, as popular author Dorothy Hann noted, sometimes it was the country girls who had never ventured further than their village street and camping was just as novel and challenging for them as for their city sisters. For poorer companies, even a weekend under canvas in somebody's garden was an exciting change in routine, and an opportunity to practise some of the new skills they had learnt, from constructing furniture from twigs and branches, to tracking, signalling, open-air cookery, and – maybe best of all – the camaraderie of the camp-fire at the end of the day.

> During the following week the Whittam Guides had the time of their lives. Into their quiet and somewhat monotonous existence the advent of these noisy, laughter-loving London girls brought a new zest and sense of adventure.
>
> It was the camp-fire scenes that thrilled them most. Never before had they known the fun of sitting round a wood-fire with the blue smoke curling upwards, shouting gaily all the songs they knew and drinking cocoa, while the shadows crept up over the hills and the stars came out one by one. The world seemed suddenly to them a new and enchanting place, full of friendly souls who greeted them as sisters just because they were Guides, and accepted them as one of themselves with none of the usual preliminaries to friendship.

(From *Peg-Lieutenant* by Mrs A. C. Osborn Hann)

Mrs A. C. Osborn Hann 1883-1963

Dorothy Hann was a prolific author of Guide fiction, and she knew what she was talking about, being involved in Guiding from about 1915 when the 5th Southwark Company was formed at her husband's church in Camberwell. When they moved to Walworth she became Captain of the 12th Southwark Rangers 1921-26, upon whom she based her popular "Peg" series, where the company features as the semi-fictional 32nd Southwarks.

There are eight books featuring Peg, beginning with *Peg's Patrol*, and following her progress as Guide and Guider, written between 1923-32. In addition there are several other stories featuring different Guides in the Company, in particular Rhoda and "Smiler".

These girls are real Walworth girls and Mrs Hann portrays them convincingly: they use Cockney slang, wit and humour, come from poor families and go out to "business" at 14 or 15. During the series Peg goes to live in Somerset to recover from an accident and eventually settles there, beginning Guides for the village girls (The Hanns also moved to Somerset and she was Captain of 1st Redhill 1925-1932). In the series, the Walworth girls often visit Peg and friendships grow between the country girls and town girls. Mrs Hann's books must have provided a real contrast to the early middle-class Guiding books set in boarding schools, like *Terry the Girl Guide*. They were illustrated with photographs of real Guides taken with Mrs Hann's Kodak camera.

She was later Captain of 1st Newton Longville Guides (1932-33) and District Commissioner for Bletchley 1932-35. The series: Peg's *Patrol, Peg the Ranger, Peg Lieutenant, Captain Peg, Peg and Her Company, Peg Junior, Peg's Babies* and *What Happened to Peg*. Also: *Rhoda the Rebel, Smiler, a Girl Guide* and *The Sunshine Shop*.

Here in the Midlands, many a Guide had never even been to the seaside before going to camp. 2nd Mansfield Company went to Chapel St. Leonards in August 1920. It was a long and tiring journey:

they spent several hours in two locked railway compartments in a siding at Lincoln, were then hitched onto the end of a train to Willoughby Station, and from there conveyed to camp in two hay-carts (a journey of three uncomfortable hours), but it was worth it!

> "Many of the guides had never seen the sea and I believe thought they ought to see it as soon as they landed at camp; they could scarcely believe that those sand hills in front of the camp was all that separated us from the mighty ocean.
> Captain gave permission for us to take a short stroll on the beach... off we went, over the sand hills and oh! The look on the guides faces as they stood up there & looked down at the sea! They then raced down the other side & began to pick shells & touch the sand just to make sure it was really there!"   (Log book of 2nd Mansfield Co.)

The above extract gives a very lively and immediate impression of camp life. The keeping of company log books was encouraged, and thank goodness because many have survived with detailed accounts of company activities, photographs and names which have greatly helped in putting together this book. The accompanying article appeared in *The Guider*, November 1929, and Nottinghamshire Girl Guides certainly seem to have taken it to heart.

Log Books

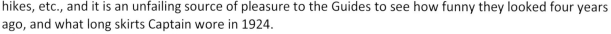

When you sit down to write your Company Log Book, you should aim at making it both business-like and artistic – two qualities not popularly supposed to go together.

There is nothing like a properly kept Log Book for bringing back happy recollections of past camps, hikes, etc., and it is an unfailing source of pleasure to the Guides to see how funny they looked four years ago, and what long skirts Captain wore in 1924.

Added to this it is a great help to a new captain who has to take over, if she has a record of the past history and traditions of the company; so in writing your Log bear in mind the impression it will give to your successor.

Again, Log Books are of great use on those devastating evenings when Commissioner comes to visit the company, and only one Leader turns up (and that one out of uniform). "Would Madam like to see the Log?" we inquire, pressing it firmly into her hand. Madam would – and should it prove sufficiently enthralling, we have time to pull ourselves together, quell the more turbulent members of the company with a stern look, and get through Roll-Call drill more or less unobserved, so that when Commissioner lays down the book, and comes back to consciousness of the present company, the Guides are all standing in neat rows ready to be inspected, and the worse is over.

Most of us love our books and look on them as friends, and the Log Book is no exception, for it is well worth cultivating, and improves greatly on acquaintance.

Elton Camp Site

Nottinghamshire Guides camped far and wide, travelling as far afield as Scotland and the Lake District, as well as camping locally whenever they could. But in 1930 they acquired a dedicated camp site of their own just off the Elton to Orston road. The site, which until about 1920, had been used for gypsum extraction (known locally as The Plaster Pits), was presented to the Girl Guides Association on payment of a nominal 1/- rent, by Lieut.-Colonel N. G. Pearson, who had purchased the land in 1928. Elton camp site was duly blessed and opened on 14th August 1930 by the Bishop of Southwell.

Lady Readett-Bayley wrote in her Annual Report:

> "The outstanding feature of the year has been the wonderful gift of 17 acres of land and a beautiful building for the use of the Guides in bad weather, by Colonel N. Gervis Pearson of Bramcote. This is the beginning of what we hope will be the finest permanent Guide camp site in England. It is situated at Elton and is easily accessible by rail. Colonel Pearson has also provided twelve tents and ground-sheets, put up a windmill to pump drinking water, and made a bathing place which is safe for both swimmers and non-swimmers. The value of the gift to the County cannot be estimated, but we hope that many future generations of children will find great happiness and much benefit from it. The Camp was opened in August by the Lord Bishop of Southwell who also came and planted a tree on November 22nd when the Guides planted an avenue of 200 poplar trees to make a fitting approach to the camp."

Bishop, Col. & Mrs Pearson, Lady R-B and Ruth Quibell(?)

"Lucky Girl Guides!" wrote a local journalist who attended the opening. He described in detail the purpose-built accommodation on the site, which had been christened "The Magpie's Nest" after some magpies which happened to be nesting nearby:

"It would be utterly wrong to call the building provided for the Guides a hut, for it is a most artistically designed and commodious building, with plenty of window-doors, so that the whole of either of the two large rooms can be thrown open to the outside air if so desired, and in addition to a very nice officers' room, there is also a store and cloakroom for Guides kit and tents when not in use. The Bishop, in unlocking the door, said he felt sure the camp and building would be of the greatest benefit to Guides throughout the country."

Demolition!

Bishop Mosley came back on a windy day in November later that year to witness the planting of the avenue of poplar trees, but also to oversee some wholesale demolition. Three 40ft high chimneys left over from the site's industrial past were due to be pulled down for safety reasons and, under professional supervision, Bishop and Guides were more than happy to accomplish the task!

EYEWITNESS: Mary Nix

"I was there when the chimneys were pulled down. There had been a brickworks on the site and the small buildings had been knocked down but the chimneys left standing. It was thought the Guides of the county might like the job, so notices were sent out, "If you want to help, just come and bring your own food." At the appointed time long ropes had been fixed round the chimneys and then laid across the field and as many girls as could get a hand on it were organised by the men in charge, and at he signal, we pulled in a giant "tug-of-war" with the chimneys and of course, we won."

It seems amazing to us today that Guides were allowed to participate in such a dangerous procedure, but it must have been a lot of fun!

Mary also recalled a later stay at Elton:

"We had a weekend at Elton in March and slept indoors because of the heavy rain. I was training for Lieutenant. Edith Parkinson was in charge and we two slept in the officer's room. On the wall was a blue print of the Artesian well and how to fix the rudder if the wind got rough. We were wakened in the night by the lashing rain and a howling gale. Rain was splashing on the girls who were lying with their heads to the window wall and they had to move to the middle of the room. Edith and I put on macs, wellies and sou'wester and with the aid of torches went across to the well to stop the pump by fixing the rudder. If you wanted to go to Elton, either for a day or weekend you first had to make your arrangements with the County Camp Advisor – Miss Francis, and Dorothy Downing who was in charge of equipment you might want to use. The key for the Magpie's Nest was held by the Elton Station Master and we had to knock on his door and ask for it and sign the book. You had to take it back before getting on the train for home."

> *This camp stands high in God's great out of doors,*
> *Cleansed and refreshed by wind, rain and sun.*
> *Ye who would lodge here strive to keep it so*
> *That naught but good may here be said or done,*
> *For we must see that nothing but the best*
> *May enter in or leave the **Magpies' Nest**.*
>
> (Inscribed on a panel at Elton by Agnes Boden)

The following year camp wardens were appointed, a company of Rangers who would be responsible for over-seeing and maintaining the hut, The Magpies Nest, throughout the year. 2nd Nottingham (Old Radford) Rangers under Miss Dorothy Gem were the first team to undertake this task, and were distinguished by wearing black and white ties. They were allowed 5/- per month for travelling expenses and would visit the camp every fortnight, to scrub the floors, clean the windows and report any damage, ensuring the site was always spick and span and ready for use.

2nd Nottingham (St Peter's, Old Radford) Rangers 1931-33

The Committee continued to look for ways to improve the amenities – including whether an outdoor latrine should be made with a penny-in-the-slot machine on the door! This could have seriously increased the 1/- each Guide paid for a week's camping, and was, thankfully, not implemented!

On 24th July 1933 the Committee reported that Colonel Pearson had now formally handed over the camp and its surrounding property to the Girl Guides Association of the county as a gift, with Lady Readett-Bayley, Sir Lancelot Rolleston and Miss Boden as trustees. Elton was to become – and still is - a wonderful resource for Guiding in the County and many former Guides and Guiders remember spending time there with great affection.

The Log Book of 17th Nottingham Rangers, kept by Edith Blagg, contains fascinating accounts of some of the earliest camps. The following entries are typical and date from Whitsuntide 1933, when the weather, for once, was "a scorcher"!

> Saturday P.M.
> "Hurrah! Elton at last. We all struggle out of the train with our cases, and kit bags, and wend our way out of the station, along the dusty road, and through a wooden gate marked "Private" and along the long drive to the Magpie's Nest. What a relief to be able to get into the shelter, and relieve ourselves of our packs. We have a walk round to see if the dear old Nest has altered at all, till Captain suggests hoisting the Union Jack, as it is the King's birthday. We struggled with the big one. Now everyone is ready for work. We've all dressed as campers, and the flag is flying, so we struggle with our tents and work hard till we have them up then we thankfully accept tea, and have a rest for an hour, then continue with the food work, then we had a stroll round the camp, have supper, and then bed. How tired and hot we all are. Goodnight."

The weather was so hot on this occasion that the girls were hard put to find anywhere to keep cool, and one Guide fainted in the heat. It was too hot to do much except sit on a grassy knoll dubbed "the mountain" and watch the trains go past – an occupation which was to prove extremely fortuitous:

> Sunday
> "We spent a lot of leisure time sitting there waving to the trains (please don't call us babies). We talked of all kinds of things, and then took our Guide Captain back to her bus, then we came home for supper, and then had a camp fire. We sang hymns and solemn camp songs. The owl joined in two or three times. We went to bed about 10.30 & so ended our first full day at Elton."

> Monday
> "We came to our "mountain" and got into our favourite positions, excursion trains were speeding through so we "babies" had quite a good time till someone yelled, "fire", and we all ran round trying to find shovels, etc. with which to fight the fires, for the last express had left 4 or 5, all along the bank. Gee, it was hot but we fought on and on, and when we had done our good deed we disposed of our shovels and sat down in our usual places, for about 10 minutes, and along came another train and did the same thing, so we stood on 'Guard' all the morning till dinner time."

Note how the girls deal so efficiently with the emergency, and record it with typical nonchalance!

On Tuesday the anonymous log-keeper finishes her report on the train going home:
> "We all walked down to the station & parted there. I was the only one going by train, the others were all cycling. As I passed the Nest, it looked deserted, and I had no one to wave to me from the hill so after securing a comfortable seat I sat thinking of all the week in front of

us. Work, and no Magpie's Nest, roll on holidays so we can have another rollicking good time!"

The entry ends with a poem:

There is a place called the Magpie's Nest
Just outside Elton station,
Where all Girl Guides go down to rest,
And change their vocation.
They become an army strong and bold
Who dig & cook like knights of old
Who keep the Nest and fields in trim,
And when the evening comes & night draws in,
We pray to God to keep from sin,
And lead us from all kind of dangers,
The 17th Nottingham Rangers.

17th Nottm. Rangers swimming in the Elton pool

11. A post-card from Wray Camp

A post card of Ambleside was recently discovered, quite by chance, in the author's family album, which revealed the identity of an anonymous scribe in one of Edith Blagg's marvellous Log Books which are held in the archives at Girlguiding Nottinghamshire.

My father's cousin, Dorothy Watkins known as "Bobbie", sent the post-card on 10th August 1931 from the Girl Guide Camp, Wray Castle, Ambleside, to her grandmother, Mrs Annie Dexter, and Aunts Annie and Maggie at 25, Portland Road, Nottingham:

> "Dear old Sunshine,
> This life just suits me. We went hiking & climbing one day, & got lost in the hills. Toured four lakes on a lorry on Tuesday, & swam in Derwent Water. (Just suit you!) We've had lovely weather, till Friday, when it was a case of taking up our beds, and walking through wet grass at 1.40 am, as the heavens opened. Sweet love to you, and daughters Anne and Magdalene, Your affec. Granddaughter, Dorothy."

17th Nottm. Rangers touring the Lakes in Mr Pooley's lorry

It soon became clear that Bobbie was camping with the 17th Nottingham Rangers and her distinctive handwriting was easily recognisable as one of the keepers of the daily log. From this record, we learn that the escapade in the hills took place on Monday 3rd August and was rather more serious than Bobbie's light hearted post card indicates! One of her fellow Rangers wrote:

"...we chose what hill we thought would be an easy one to ascend, but looks were deceiving. At times we were lost in the bracken, it being so tall, at other times we were walking on ground that was like a sponge. Having consulted the map & found out that we were on Lough Rigg Fell, we tried to find our bearings to enable us to get back to camp, but like the "Babes in the Wood" we were lost. Twelve lonely Rangers lost on the mountains, what a tragedy! We decided that we should not like to stay out all night, so led by one adventurous spirit, namely Bobbie, we started to descend... and we found our way back to the road."

On August 13th it was Bobbie's turn to report:

WE HIKE TO CONISTON

"It had been pre-arranged that we should hike to Coniston to-day, so when we tumbled out of our disordered bedclothes, and found the smiling sun beaming down on our little corner of the world, we were highly elated, and danced a little war dance – till I fell over a tent peg! After an invigorating cold water wash, we broke our fast, doing justice to our Cooks' efforts. Then we went about our various duties, and dinner was cut and packed up in rucksacks for us to carry, Edna and Daisy stalking off with the oranges. (They weren't green, were they?) – That is to say, Edna and Daisy weren't green, - not the oranges. Captain left before us, as she had to call at Ambleside. She would meet us at either Hawkshead or Coniston. As she departed, she called to Miss Wilson to bring something along with her. Miss W. Didn't quite catch what she said. Thought it was "Mac". Accordingly she entered the officers' tent to collect some, but no mac could she find. A search was made high and low, but it refused to be found, so giving it up as a bad job, we started on our way.

The countryside rang with the sound of our clear, tuneful, girlish voices __! For as we stalked along, we sang over, and over again, two rounds which Barbara Bell had taught us. Miss Wilson, still puzzled about the mac, wondered if it was 'mac' that Cappy said. So we said "Mac, Mat, Hat, Pack," and went through the alphabet, so to speak. Boycey, stopping in the middle of the path, yells out "MAP!!" Of course, we nearly all had a sixpenny bet that it was her map Captain wanted – not mac, so Miss Wilson trots back for it, while we walk slowly to the Lodge gates. Here we sat on a wall and recommenced our tuneful ditties. Miss Wilson was soon back, map in hand, and our little party, six in all – (namely, Litch, Nellie, Barbara, Boycey, Miss Wilson and Bob) stepped forward once more. We soon came to Mr. Kemble – the vicar's pleasant abode, and glancing through his iron gate as we passed, we espied him wheeling a huge wheelbarrow down the drive towards us. We stopped and chatted for about five minutes, and he directed us to Hawkshead over the fields, as being 'a near cut'. We were to see him again in the evening, for he was bringing a Scoutmaster to show us some Jujitsu. After cheery "goodbyes" we hopped over into the fields, and followed the footpath wither Mr K. had directed us.

We stepped briskly out, swinging our sticks, & singing, whistling, chatting and laughing. And well we might. It was a topping day, and Nature looked her best. We went through some lovely scenery. It was good to be alive! At last we reached Hawkshead. Dear little place, with quaint old cottages overhanging narrow, winding, cobbled streets, with splashes of colour here and there, where gay Nasturtiums, and many coloured cottage posies fringed the houses. Turning a corner, what should we see but our friend Mr Pooley's lorry, and out of a little garage near by, we soon espied the ever smiling face of the said Mr Pooley.... We chatted for a while with him, and he also directed a way to us by the fields and Tarn, then we went on our way once more. We climbed up hill and down dale at a brisk pace, Nellie and Barbara bringing up the rear occasionally until they found a place which sold 'pop', and they both discovered they were thirsty, so they stayed behind to regale themselves, while we four strong minded people – plodded on.

We were about two miles from Coniston when Litch stopped & exclaimed, "O look at this!" Whereupon we looked. And there was a snake, about a foot in length, basking at the side of the road. Someone prodded it with her stick and it shot off into the undergrowth, and was hidden. He must have been a grass snake. It wasn't very long after, that we espied the lake gleaming in the sun below us. We reached Coniston in record time, and kept an eye open for Captain, and Daisy and Edna, for we needed dinner, as the 'inner man' was clamouring a little. – Still, we four were carrying the grub! Rounding a bend, we came upon Cappy walking to meet us. We turned back to sit in a field which led to the Lake, and higher up the road were Nellie and Barbara. They were by no means slow in overtaking us. Perhaps the 'pop' had stimulated them. – Or, would it be something stronger than pop? No, I hardly think so. We flopped down in the grass of the field and then realised how tired we were, as well as hungry. Capn. said we could start the eats without the late comers, which we accordingly did, and ate heartily. Then we were thirsty, and where were the oranges? Of course, Daisy and Edna were carrying the lot with them. And wherever were they? Would they never come? But lo! Here they come, with a high old tale about getting over a wall and losing themselves or something. Still, the oranges were more important just then, so we made them tip 'em up. – (They were all intact.)

We stayed in this field for some time, resting, writing, and indulging in a bit of friendly banter with each other, till Captain thought it would be a good idea to buy tea in Coniston and then set off campwards, and be quite ready for 'the Jujitsu man' when we arrived back. So we got upon our feet once more, collected our goods and chattels and went in search of tea. We found a cottage, and asked to have tea in the garden, but all the tables were occupied or some such tale, so we had to have it in a stuffy room. We were stifled! Tea over, we donned our macs, those who had them, as it rained. (Captain had hers, by the way!) and waited for the bus. We got in the bus, and it packed to overflowing. On the way back, Barbara, and Edna had to get near the windows. – In case of emergency, y'know. They had a very unpleasant feeling of nausea, to put it politely. Still, nothing eventful happened – on the journey home.

Alighting from the 'bus, we had nearly three miles to traverse back to camp, and it was about 5.30, and the Vicar & S.M. were coming at 6.0pm. Gosh! We'd have to hurry! And we did. But when we reached Camp, there was no sign of either of them. But we went up to Wray Castle eventually and found the Vicar, and Mr Fox the S.M. who showed us Jujitsu tricks for the rest of the evening. It was great fun. One or two of us ached in various places for some day after!

After this strenuous exercise we were ready for supper. Then, weary, worn, but glad, we slipped into our then well made, welcome bedclothes. Here endeth the second Thursday."

17th Nottm. Rangers at camp. Bobbie is 2nd from R. Who are the others?

Aug. 14th 1931 Friday

WE TRY TO PACK

"Our last day! And when we rose early, we found a grey morning. We were disappointed for we had hoped for a gloriously hot, sunny day to give the final touches to our brown skins. But our hopes were not to materialise. Still we couldn't grumble for we had been awfully lucky in the weather. I was Cook today along with Litch, and we soon had the fire blazing merrily, the porridge boiling, kettle singing, and bacon burning. Oh no! Not quite. To tell you the truth, I think we cooked it very well. (Believe it, or believe it not). After we had breakfasted well and happily, the usual duties were performed, and then came the sad task of striking Camp. Sob sob! Down came the Bell Tents and the little Ridge Tents, and packed. Tent pegs scraped and packed. Only the Store tent, and Kitchen Roof were left up as long as possible. We worked hard, all day. It was hot even without the sun. The cooks had been seeing to dinner in between whiles, and we did justice to it for our work had created an appetite. We had cooked Irish Stew and Jam Dumplings. Really they were top hole, you know. Ask Nellie if you don't believe me! After this diversion we were ready for work once more, and recommenced with a will. We were going to Ambleside at 6 o'clock to see Miss Wilson off to her home in Ireland. Miss W., (thoughtful soul) as she was boiling an egg to take with her in the train, thought she would boil the eggs also, ready for our homeward journey to-morrow. Which she did, and carefully separated them from the uncooked eggs that we were having for breakfast in the morning. Bless her!

Half past five, and still at work packing. We fly to get cleaned, and by six, we are off down to the ferry, bound for Ambleside, with our dear Q.M., Miss Wilson. This was the last time we crossed Lake Windermere. It was a jolly crossing. There was some time left, so we ambled side by side round the Ambleside shops, and purchased rock, and fudge and candy, and small souvenirs of Lakeland, and took a long, last look of the pretty place. Meanwhile, Miss Wilson was on a quiver to be off, and there was still time to spare before the bus came in to take her to Windermere Station. But even then she had to run for it as it appeared from nowhere and was sailing away without her! We all flew after it, gesticulating wildly, all but calm Captain. Miss W. sprang inside the bus, but made the driver wait, till she had said 'Good-bye' properly to each of us, in turn, and then they carried her off, and we waved till she was out of sight. Now we turned Campwards, one member less of our company, and stepped out briskly, for we had a good three miles in front of us, and supper to get ready on arrival, and we mustn't be in bed late tonight, as we have to be "up betimes" on the morrow! We had a topping walk back, and supper was welcome at the end of it, - but, by jove! Bed was! Here endeth the Second Friday."

The matter of the boiled eggs is recounted the following day by another log-keeper...

"...after breakfast (boiled eggs, which everyone remarked seemed very hard boiled)...
   [Later, on the train] we had hardy settled down, when someone mentioned eating... out came the eggs & bread & butter, gee! One didn't realise how hungry one was until the grub was brought into view. Next followed the job of holding bread in one hand and cracking eggs with the other. Suddenly there was a yell of despair, someone's egg wasn't hard- boiled, then a shriek of dismay, someone's wasn't cooked! We looked at each other, was it possible that they had never been in water... one lot had been cooked twice and now we had raw eggs and bread and butter for dinner. It was no use crying over spilt milk, so we ate what we had and vowed to get out at the next station and buy bananas."

Miss Hackett, Miss Daniels and Miss Wilson led the Wray Camp; "Boycey" was Nellie Boyce, but so far, most of Bobbie's fellow campers remain unidentified. Were you one of them?

Dorothy Eva Watkins (1911-1998) was aged 20 in 1931. She was the sister of "Desperate Dan" cartoonist, Dudley Watkins, and a competent artist in her own right. She joined the ATS in the Second World War and subsequently worked as a graphic artist and painter. In 1970 she emigrated to America, where she married Senator Arthur Watkins and died in 1998.

12. Coming of age, 1932

The "coming of age", or 21st birthday of the Girl Guide movement, was scheduled for 1931, but such was the economic state of the country that celebrations were postponed until the following year. Anyone who can do their arithmetic is aware that Guiding was well underway before 1910, and that the celebration was already overdue. No matter! It was time for a nationwide party to honour the achievements of the many Guides and Guiders who had brought the movement thus far.

At the brand-new Headquarters at 19, Buckingham Palace Road, London, two reunion tea-parties were attended by Princess Louise, Miss Agnes Baden-Powell, Margaret Macdonald, Miss Helen Malcolm of the YWCA Guides and many others who had been there at the very beginning.

"Guide Week" was 22-29 May 1932, when all companies and packs and individuals set out to do extra good turns. For example, 3rd Ollerton Girl Guides put on a special event for 40 old people at Ollerton WI Hall, doing all the catering and serving themselves. Other companies collected eggs for the hospitals and toys and books for disadvantaged children. Sunday of that week was Church Parade and across the county Guides marched proudly to their parish churches. In Nottingham city centre the whole of the Forest Division participated, with more that 1000 Guides at St Mary's Church in the Lace Market, 700 Brownies at St Peter's, and another 300 Guides at Castle Gate Congregational Chapel. As the three services ended, some 2,000 girls converged and marched past the Council House where the Lord Mayor, Lady Mayoress and the Bishop of Southwell took the salute. The parade was under the command of Division Commissioner Mrs Gordon, assisted by District Commissioners Miss Gem, Miss Trease, Miss Briggs, Miss Boden and Miss D. Snook (later Mrs Hanson).

In the north of the county, a combined service took place on May 29th in the Chapel at Worksop College, some 300 Guides taking part. District Commissioner Mrs Shirley, Division Commissioner Miss Barber, the Marchioness of Tichfield (President) and the Mayoress of Worksop, Mrs Longbottom, were all present. District Captain Miss Milward was responsible for the arrangements. The Rev. Dr F.J. Shirley reflected in his sermon:

> "Today you celebrate the 21st anniversary of the Girl Guide movement, which has leapt all barriers of race and colour and religion, and broken down all national frontiers … England has given a tremendous impetus in the introduction of the Girl Guide movement to other nations of the world, and this has helped towards the better understanding of people with people and to break down all those barriers that have hitherto existed. For the purpose of your move - ment is not national, but international. It is to be one of the factors in this 20th Century… true internationalism is the only possible solution for the world's future."

He went on to suggest,

"If the Guide movement has counted that much in the force of the whole world, consider what you yourselves, each one individually, must count in your smaller divisions, districts and parishes."

Southwell Minster, June 11th 1932

Westgate, Guides as far as the eye can see!

The grand climax of the birthday celebrations was a gathering of some 4,000 Guides at Southwell Minster, where two services, one following immediately on the heels of the other, had to be held to accommodate them all. The Nottingham and District Guides went first, followed by the County Guides. Lady Readett-Bayley took the salute at the West Gate and the service began with the presentation of the colours of the 28 districts followed by the National Anthem.

  The Bishop, Dr Mosley, referred in his address to the economic depression of the time, saying that he believed they should come through it because of what the Scouts and Guides stood for:

"To love God, and to follow the Great Guide – Jesus Christ Himself.

"To love your Country - which also meant friendship with other nations and peace with the world.

"To love Home, courage, kindness, truth, honour."

He said he liked to think that they would look back on these dark days and say, "Yes, it was then – England – it was then she undertook her work for God among the nations of the world."

The Camp Fire at Norwood Park – Miss Nettleship conducts the singing

After the services the Guides marched to Norwood Park where they had tea, followed by a Great Camp Fire under the leadership of Miss Ursula Nettleship from London. Miss Nettleship was a prominent member of the Council for the Encouragement of Music and the Arts and a friend of Benjamin Britten, so it must have been quite a *coup* to secure her services for the occasion. In spite of heavy thunder, the gathering was judged a huge success with marching and singing in which the Bishop and Provost joined.

Main party L-R: Mrs & Col. Starkey, Miss Nettleship, Mrs Dowson (Plains Division Commissioner), Lady Readett-Bayley, Mrs Conybeare (Southwell Division Commissioner), Mrs Gordon (Forest Division Commissioner), Canon Jackson and Provost Conybeare with Ben the dog!

The Ring of Adventurers

Throughout the birthday celebrations, the Editor of *The Guide*, "Captain" Vera Marshall, travelled the country in a red Morris car called Gulliver, meeting Guides at a series of semi-impromptu camp-fire rings. The venue would be announced beforehand in the magazine and Guides would make their own way there on the day. The Ring of Adventurers came to Wollaton Park, Nottingham, on July 9th.

> "Some adventurous spirits had hiked eight miles and were hiking back after the Ring; others had bicycled from Derby; others walked or bussed from Nottingham and neighbouring villages. Ooh, it was hot! But very, very lovely, and we were so specially glad to have several of the Nottingham Post Guides and Rangers with us. It was really sporting of them to come all the way to the Ring, and several walked long distances across the Park on crutches. Here again, the general public joined the outskirts of the Ring, and judging by their faces they were thoroughly intrigued with the singing...
>
> The heat and the long treks did not stop the Nottinghamshire Guides from singing like true adventurers and many new songs were exchanged.

A Hundred Years Ago

We have Miss Boden, District Commissioner for South Nottingham, to thank for having obtained permission to light a fire in Wollaton Park, for this is not really allowed. We had a grand fire; Miss Boden must have smiled very Guidily upon the Park keepers. The evening had several small adventures. At one moment during the Ring a frog caused a diversion, and leapt all over some of the Guides, eventually vanishing right up one poor Guider's skirt. He was rescued, however, and carried away to safety.

After the Ring, Gulliver refused to leave the Park. The Park officially closed at 9.30 pm, but this did not perturb Gulliver, and he needed quite a considerable amount of coaxing and bribing before he would budge... However, he eventually responded to our coaxes, and finally carried nine or ten of the adventurers all the way through the Park to the gates. We camped again outside Nottingham and then Gulliver sped back to London on Sunday in grilling heat, having had the most exciting and best week-end he has had for a long time."
(*The Guide*, July 23 1932)

At the time of these celebrations, there were 247 companies in Nottinghamshire, 654 Guiders, 4,388 Girl Guides (including 23 Lones), 930 Rangers, 25 Cadets and 2,621 Brownies.

INDEX

Photographs

Unless stated below, all unattributed photographs
in the text are the property of
Girlguiding Nottinghamshire or Girlguiding UK.

Cover photo (unknown Guide) - Eileen Harvey
p.4 (vintage postcard) - property of the author
p.10 - Ivy Chilvers
p.12 (lower) - Eileen Foster
p.17 (Duchess of Portland) - the author
p.18 - Peter Blatherwick
p.21 (Trease memorial) -the author
p. 22 - Jane Robinson
pp. 30 & 31 - Collingham & District L. H. S.
p.35 - Sue Davies
p.42 (lower) -Pam Fogg
p.48 - Chris Hawthorne
p.68 - the author
pp.70, 71 & 72 all by H. Barrett of Southwell, 1932